Using Bitcoin

Three Guides to the World's
First Cryptocurrency

Bitcoin: A Simple Introduction

Understanding Bitcoin

And

Bitcoin: A Concise History

by

Eric Morse

Bitcoin:
A Simple Introduction

By

Eric Morse

To Alice and Bob, who do not appear anywhere in this book.

Table of Contents

Introduction: Who Is This Book For?

<u>Bitcoin: A Simple Introduction</u> is an entry-level primer for new users. The intended audience for this book is someone who has just heard about Bitcoin and has only a vague (and perhaps flawed) notion of what it is. Maybe they heard about it from an excited friend who wants them to invest. Maybe they heard it from a customer that has asked them to start accepting Bitcoin for payment. Maybe they saw a headline in a financial magazine or heard it in a keynote speech at a conference. Or perhaps they saw a "Bitcoin" button as an option when buying something online. Wherever they came across it, Bitcoin is now in their circle of awareness. It is an itch that needs to be scratched. The flame of curiosity has been kindled and they want to know more.

Sadly, the first sources of information these people are likely to come across aren't meant for them. They are meant for developers or academics or IT professionals. These books go into great detail about concepts that are both irrelevant and confusing to the average new user. There is nothing wrong with these books, but they are not what the new or perspective Bitcoin user needs. These people are not developers. They are not cryptographers. They don't work in IT. To them, the words "private key" and "hard fork" are physical objects that have nothing to do with computers or software. And "hashrate" is just flat out gibberish. The Bitcoin community goes out of its way to teach people new meanings for these words, and that is a mistake. People don't want to learn a new language. They don't want to learn about encryption or other concepts that have no point of reference in their everyday activities. They just want to know what all this "Bitcoin" fuss is about.

This book is for them.

It is not a detailed technical examination of code and concepts. Nor is it a step-by-step tutorial of how to back up a wallet or mine bitcoin. It is an explanation in everyday language of what Bitcoin is, how it works, and what makes it special. It contains no technical jargon. I avoid even the "correct" names for concepts if those names would be confusing or unfamiliar. For example, I use the phrase "public ledger" much more often than "Blockchain", and refer to "hashrate" as "computing power" in the rare instances where I mention it at all. The words "cryptocurrency" and "private key" do not appear in this text outside of this introduction.

Yes, I over-simplify some concepts and ignore others if they are beyond what a new user needs to know or is likely to ask. I use some flawed but "accurate-enough" analogies and examples that may make experienced Bitcoin enthusiasts cringe.

All of this is intentional. Every improper term or contrived example is a decision made for the sake of simplicity.

Likewise, I kept the style of the book light and informal, with a question-and-answer format that is more appealing than the rigid format of a textbook. While this may invite people to skip to whatever question they have at the moment, but the book should be read from start to finish. Some of the answers to questions later in the book expand on answers to earlier ones.

For the target audience: I hope you find this book useful and enjoyable. For the more experienced reader: I hope you remember what it was like to be a newbie and understand the trade-offs I've made. You may not be the target audience, but your boss, your lawyer, and the guy running the register at the coffee shop almost certainly are. I hope you find this book informative enough to consider buying them a copy.

Thank You In Advance For Reading.

Eric Morse

What Is Bitcoin?

Is it a currency? Is it a computer program?

Short answer: Bitcoin is a way to send, receive, and store value on the internet without the involvement or permission of banks, payment processors, or other third parties. If you're thinking this sounds a lot like cash, you're right. Bitcoin is, among other things, cash for the internet.

Long Answer: When someone says the word "Bitcoin" they could be referring to one of several related concepts. Yes, Bitcoin (BTC) is a currency much like the US Dollar (USD) or the Euro (EUR). You can spend it. You can save it. However, there are some interesting and substantial differences between Bitcoin and these other currencies, and we'll discuss some of those throughout the book.

Bitcoin is also a method for tracking ownership of currency by updating globally distributed ledger. There's a lot of meaning in that last sentence, so let's break it down. If you have a bank account, the bank is keeping track of how much money you have in it. They keep the ledger. You're probably keeping own ledger as well, but the bank has your money, so theirs is the one that matters in this example. When you buy something for ten dollars with your debit card, your bank removes ten dollars from their ledger and the merchant's bank adds ten dollars to theirs. Now imagine that instead of multiple banks with multiple ledgers, there was only one bank with one ledger. When you buy something, the one bank that both you and the merchant share updates its one ledger, showing that ten dollars have changed ownership from you to the merchant. Now erase the bank and replace it with a network of computers communicating over the internet. Instead of representing Dollars or Euros, values in the ledger are called bitcoins. That is the Bitcoin network.

Note: Since the same word refers to both the currency and the computer network, I will use "Bitcoin" (note the capital "B") when referring to the network, and "bitcoin" (lowercase) when talking about the unit of currency. Also, the abbreviation "BTC" always refers to the currency, never to the network.

What Is The Blockchain?

The ledger mentioned above has a name: the Blockchain. The name comes from the way it is maintained. Transactions are not written individually, but in blocks or collections of many transactions. The Bitcoin blockchain is:

Complete. It contains every Bitcoin transaction ever made, all the way back to the very first one.

Unchangeable. I hesitate to use the word "impossible", but it is extremely difficult to modify a Bitcoin transaction once it has been written to the ledger. Not only that, but every block of transactions makes harder to change the blocks that came before it. If a transaction has over six blocks written on top of it, it is essentially unchangeable.

Public. The Blockchain is not secret; anyone can view it and its contents online. Does this mean that people can view your Bitcoin transactions? Yes. You can look up any Bitcoin transaction (even ones that aren't yours) and see related transactions which came before and after it. However, the only information in the ledger is Bitcoin addresses (consider them to be like account numbers for now), transaction IDs, timestamps and amounts. You do not see names or items purchased. You do not see information that would allow you to assume someone's identity or conduct transactions using their money. You just see a record of BTC moving from one set of addresses to another.

Distributed. There isn't just one copy of the Bitcoin ledger tucked away on a server. There are thousands of copies, each identical (and kept that way by the network).

What Is Mining?

Every computer that is properly connected to the Bitcoin network is a node. Nodes relay transactions, hold a full copy of the public ledger, and can also be used as Bitcoin wallets. But not every node is equal.

Some members of the network are engaged in the crucial task of "confirming" or writing transactions to the ledger. These special nodes are called Miners. The nature of the work they are performing is both complex and difficult... so much so that it requires specialized hardware to perform efficiently. However, these miners aren't performing this work out of the goodness of their hearts. The Bitcoin network compensates them in two ways for every block of transactions they write to the ledger:

1. They receive the transaction fees contained in that block of transactions
2. They receive a mining reward of 25 BTC. This amount goes down every few years, and will eventually reach zero, forcing miners to rely solely on transaction fees for income.

Miners are competing with one another to confirm the next block of transactions. Since mining is so difficult, most miners join "pools" that combine their computing power and split any rewards they earn.

Can anyone mine? Is it profitable?

Technically, yes, anyone can mine. There is nothing stopping you from installing the Bitcoin software on your PC and joining the network as a miner. However, the likelihood of you mining a block (and getting the associated rewards) is vanishingly small. You'd essentially be wasting your time and electricity.
Why is this? The Bitcoin network is designed to confirm (or mine) a block of transactions every ten minutes on average. There is a certain amount of computing power required to make this happen... but if the mining power of the network exceeds that, then the difficulty of mining increases to compensate, thus maintaining the 10-minute average. The more people mine, the harder mining becomes. In the early days, people could mine with the CPU in their desktop computers. As Bitcoin became more popular and more people started mining, the difficulty increased to the point that mining with CPUs became too hard. Then people started using their PC graphics cards (which are much more powerful) to earn the mining rewards. After that, companies began producing specialized hardware for mining. Now we are at a point where there have been multiple generations of this specialized hardware, each much more powerful than the last. Yes, mining is still profitable, but unless you can afford to invest in expensive hardware and have a cheap (or free) source of electricity, mining is not rewarding for the average person.

What about Cloud Mining? What is it and is it profitable?

Mining hardware is not only expensive, but it needs to be replaced with newer hardware often to keep up with the rising difficulty. Add to this the cost of electricity to run and cool the hardware. Most people can't afford it.

But what if you could rent it?

At first glance, cloud mining seems like a great solution. Since you can't afford all the mining hardware yourself, you contract with someone else who has some they're willing to share. You lease their extra computing power and they run it for you at their facility, which is usually located somewhere where electricity is cheap. When the term of the lease (typically one year) is up, you can terminate the contract, continue it, or upgrade it so you have access to even more computing power. All the while, you are earning BTC with the computing power you leased.

Most people who get into these contracts fail to profit substantially (or at all). The cloud mining companies may be outright scams with no (or very little) actual hardware. Or the purchaser overestimates the amount of money they can earn with their leased equipment and ends up with little (or even negative) profit at the end of the term. Those that profit typically only do so due to the increase in the value of BTC over the lease term. If you're going to profit from increasing value, you'd be better off just buying BTC on an exchange and holding it instead of investing in mining (cloud or otherwise).

So is it really too late to make good money mining Bitcoin?

If you don't have access to serious start-up capital, Yes. BTC mining has evolved beyond the ability of most people to participate. It is an industry now, with startup costs worthy of that status.

What Is A Bitcoin Address?

Bitcoin is held in addresses, and transactions on the public ledger show BTC moving from one or more source addresses to one or more destination addresses. At first glance, each Bitcoin address seems like random numbers and letters in both upper and lowercase.

But don't worry, you don't need to memorize, recognize, or type these addresses.

If you need to send bitcoin to someone, you will either click a link that has the recipient's Bitcoin address (and sometimes the amount of BTC) embedded in it, scan a code that contains the destination address, or copy/paste the address into your Bitcoin wallet from an email, website, or other source.

If you ever find yourself manually typing a Bitcoin address into something... STOP. Something is wrong.

One comparison you will hear often is that a Bitcoin address is like a bank account number. I prefer to compare Bitcoin addresses to reloadable Visa gift cards. Each card has its own number, and none of them has your name on it. You or someone else loads a card with dollars and you spend it wherever debit/credit cards are accepted. Once you spend it all, you can either load that same card with more money and keep using it, or you can buy a new gift card with a different number and use that one instead. Now imagine you had a wallet full of these debit cards, and the ability to transfer money between them.

You go to the coffee shop and use Card #1 to buy a latte. The drink is $2.50, and the card has $25.00 on it. After the transaction, you move the remaining balance, $22.50, to Card #2. Later on, you use Card #2 to buy a magazine for $15.00. After this transaction (or, with Bitcoin, as PART of the transaction) you put the remaining $7.50 onto Card #3. This chain of transactions continues until your balance reaches zero. This is how you use Bitcoin. Each card is a Bitcoin address, and you manage the addresses with a Bitcoin wallet that allows you to make transactions and shift balances between them. Depending on the wallet, leftover funds from a transaction (the change) will return to the original Bitcoin address or be sent to a new address that is generated automatically.

What wallet should I use?

There are a lot of Bitcoin wallets to choose from. Some platforms (such as Android) have more choices than others, but wallets for your smartphone have nearly identical feature sets. Desktop wallets some additional features, but tend not to be as user-friendly. I recommend a mobile wallet for beginners. I am partial to Mycelium on Android and Breadwallet on iOS. Electrum is a good desktop wallet. If you're using another wallet, make sure it is storing data and performing the transactions on your device, not just serving as a front-end to a wallet service based in the cloud. If you're not sure how to tell, here's a hint: If you can go to a website and type a username and password to access your BTC outside of the app... don't use that service. Avoid web-based wallets.

Is Bitcoin Free To Use?

No. There are two fees that most users will encounter when using Bitcoin. The first are the fees that exchanges charge to convert dollars to bitcoin. These fees vary among the various changes, but they should not be ignored. If you are sending BTC to someone who will be converting it to USD or some other currency, you should include enough extra to cover any conversion fees. Otherwise, the $200 that you sent to grandma in Europe may end up being $170.

Now we come to transaction fees. Writing blocks of transactions to a ledger is easy. Writing blocks of transactions to a distributed public ledger in a manner that prevents them from being changed is much harder. It is so hard, in fact, that the parts of the Bitcoin network that perform this service expect to be compensated for doing it.

How much do they get? It depends on how busy they are and how complex your transaction is. Throughout Bitcoin's history, recommended transaction fees have ranged from fractions of a cent to just over a dollar per transaction. Note the use of the word "recommended". The Bitcoin network does not force you to include a minimum fee. If your wallet software allows it, you can perform transactions with no fee at all. If you do this, your transaction may take days or weeks to be written, IF it is written at all. Meanwhile, Bitcoin confirms your friend's transaction with a $.50 fee in an hour, and your other friend's transaction, with a $1.50 fee in ten minutes. This isn't meant to imply there is an exact fee-to-minutes guide you can refer to. There is not. Good Bitcoin wallets will make suggestions of fee amounts for "low priority" or "high priority" transactions. You should look for and follow those suggestions.

What happens if you forget to include a fee or include one that is too low?

The best case scenario is that your transaction will still be confirmed, but it will just take longer.... Hours (or days) instead of minutes. However, as load on the Bitcoin network increases, miners have an increasing incentive to ignore transactions that do not have adequate fees. This is how they get paid after all. Your transaction will languish in the backlog for up to fourteen days before the system cancels it and returns your BTC to you.

Does this mean that not including a fee is a way to make a Bitcoin transaction reversible?

No. The statement that Bitcoin transactions are irreversible assumes the transactions have been "confirmed" or written to the public ledger. Once that happens, they are carved in stone. But this brings up an excellent point you should consider if you will be on the receiving end of transactions. You should wait for confirmations on the network before rendering goods or services. If you cannot do that, at least verify the transaction includes an adequate fee. You can do this by viewing the transaction in your wallet.

Are there ways to increase the fee after it is sent?

Actually, yes... but these methods are a combination of Not Free, Not Guaranteed, and Not Easy.

There are Transaction accelerators services such as ViaBTC and BTC.com that will include your transaction into the next block they write to the public ledger. These services have their own criteria, such as a minimum included fee or a short period in which they accept transactions. You will need to know your Bitcoin transaction ID. The easiest way to get that is to view the transaction in your Bitcoin wallet or enter your Bitcoin address on a site like Blockchain.info. If this seems unnecessarily complicated, you can avoid having to do it by including fees.

Further up the level of complexity is creating specially-crafted transactions that reference the transaction that is "stuck" waiting to be written:

Replace By Fee (RBF) issues a new transaction (with a much higher fee) that attempts to spend the same bitcoins as the previous one in hopes that the system will replace the older transaction with the newer one. I don't recommend it.

Child Pays for Parent (CPFP) issues a new transaction (with a much higher fee) that spends the output of the "stuck" transaction in hopes that a miner will write them BOTH, as the second depends on the first.

These are brief descriptions, not instructions. You might not be able to do these on a mobile wallet, or in every circumstance. You should not try these options without asking someone more experienced or having tested them yourself with very small amounts. Preferably both.

What Makes Bitcoin Special?

Now that you know what Bitcoin is, what is all the fuss about? What are the properties of Bitcoin that make it such a big deal?

Bitcoin is Non-reversible. Unlike credit card transactions (and Paypal), Bitcoin transactions are non-reversible. Once a Bitcoin transaction has been confirmed, the BTC has permanently changed hands. Neither the sender nor any 3rd party can undo the transaction. It is the internet equivalent of handing someone a twenty dollar bill. Once the money hits the receiver's hand (or their BTC address) it is theirs. This quality of Bitcoin is a boon to merchants, who no longer have to worry about chargebacks.

Bitcoin has low fees (for some definitions of "low"). As of this writing, the current average fee is just over one dollar. By the time you read these words, it could be higher or lower, depending on the current volume of transactions and the dollar value of bitcoin. The fee for sending bitcoin can vary greatly, but it is determined by how complex the transaction is and how soon you want the transaction to be written to the ledger. It is NOT determined by distance, the number of borders that must be crossed, or the amount of BTC involved. Sending $100 worth of BTC to someone across the street costs the same as sending $100,000 to someone on the other side of the globe. However, if you want the transaction confirmed within an hour, expect to pay more than if you could wait.

Bitcoin has no mandatory 3rd Parties. If you write a check to send someone money, you do so with the permission, knowledge, and involvement of both your bank and the recipient's, not to mention the various government entities that both banks answer to. If you buy a coffee cup with a credit card, both the store's bank and payment processor are involved in the transaction. Normally these 3rd parties are transparent and beneficial. But sometimes things aren't normal. What if the store's credit card processor gets hacked? What if Visa and Mastercard stop doing business with you (as happened to Wikimedia in 2014)? What if Paypal scoops money out of your store's account due to a dispute? What if there is a misunderstanding and the IRS freezes your checking account while they clear things up? These abnormalities may be rare, but they can be extremely disruptive, even life-changing. With Bitcoin they are impossible. With Bitcoin, the involvement of 3rd parties from banks to payment processors to governments is optional. That being said, many merchants DO use a Bitcoin payment processor like BitPay or Coinbase because it is easier than setting everything up themselves. This is their choice, not a requirement.

Bitcoin is secure from interference and confiscation. This is a logical extension of the previous point, but it is worth mentioning by itself. With Bitcoin, you own and control your money as if it were physical cash in your pocket. But this cash can be used online. It can be sent across the internet, across borders, across governmental boundaries in defiance of laws, treaties, tariffs or regulations. No one can prevent you from making transactions. No one can stop you from doing business with someone your bank doesn't like or sending money somewhere the government would rather you didn't. Bitcoin cannot be seized or taken from you without your permission. Do not underestimate the importance of this. It is one of the founding concepts of Bitcoin. Bitcoin may not be free to obtain or use... but it is Free.

Bitcoin is finite. The number of bitcoins is capped at 21 million. Once that last bitcoin is created (or "mined") no government, corporation, or other entity can make more. Why is this important? Compare this quality of bitcoin to almost any other currency. The potential number of US dollars is infinite. Every year the government creates more, and in doing so it makes the existing dollars less valuable. This is why things cost more now than they did years ago, and why the money you put in your bank account today won't buy as much when you retire in a few decades. Bitcoin doesn't have this problem. While the value of bitcoin in terms of USD fluctuates, this fluctuation is not due to the production of more currency.

Bitcoin is infinitely divisible. The smallest unit of US currency is the penny, or $0.01 USD. The smallest unit of BTC is the satoshi, or 0.00000001 BTC. Bitcoin is divisible up to 8 decimal places, which *in theory* allows it to be used for very small transactions known as "micropayments." A micropayment system might allow viewers to pay for videos by the minute or for web content by the page. In practice, however, rising transaction fees make BTC less suitable for these types of tiny transactions. There are ways around this, and some proposed changes to the Bitcoin protocol might return fees to a level low enough to spur renewed interest in micropayments. Note that 8 decimal places is the CURRENT limit of divisibility. It can be increased.

Yes, there is more. Discussions of scripting, multi-signature addresses, and digital autonomous corporations are far beyond what is appropriate for an introductory text. The only thing a new or potential Bitcoin user should know about them is that Bitcoin has more potential than what you've read thus far. The Bitcoin protocol can do some strange, interesting, and very useful things. These things have little impact on how you might use Bitcoin as a new user.

Who Controls Bitcoin?

Short Answer: No one. And Everyone.

Long Answer: Bitcoin is not a product of any government, corporation, or organization. It does not have a President, CEO, or Board of Directors. Bitcoin is structured in a way that no individual or group can change how it works.

That doesn't mean that Bitcoin can't change. It can and it does. Bitcoin is updated often, but the changes are agreed upon by multiple parties, each acting as much in their own interests as the interests of the Bitcoin economy. None of these parties "control" Bitcoin on their own, but the evolution of the Bitcoin protocol occurs through their interaction:

Developers. Bitcoin is implemented in software, so it might seem that the developers are in control. If someone wanted to introduce a change to Bitcoin, could they not just influence one of the Bitcoin developers to add that change to some new version of Bitcoin? They could. But the code that runs Bitcoin, much like the distributed ledger of transactions, is public. People (developers and not) are constantly looking at the code and all the changes made to it. Any "sneaky" change that someone tried to make probably wouldn't make it out of code review, and would certainly be discovered in the testing phase that all new versions of the software undergo prior to release. But suppose someone influenced ALL (or a significant portion) of the developers? Could they get together and force a change? A change to increase the maximum number of bitcoins to 50 million, for instance? If they did, they'd have to answer to...

Miners. Miners run the machines that write the transactions to the public ledger. They get paid from the fees that users include in their transactions. If a new version of Bitcoin is released, miners must update the software on their machines in order for the changes to be implemented. Or they can just ignore it. If miners feel that the "new version" of Bitcoin will harm their business or negatively affect the price of BTC, they can reject it by simply not running it. Obviously, miners have different ideas about what is and is not good for Bitcoin so some will run the new code while others may not The code that ends up with the most computing power behind it "wins". If there is no clear winner, there may be two competing versions of Bitcoin existing side-by-side for a time.

The Network. Miners aren't the only people essential to the network. Every person running properly configured Bitcoin software on their computer is part of the network. They don't write transactions to the ledger, but they do communicate with one another to propagate those transactions across the Bitcoin network. If you buy an item online with bitcoin, your transaction will be visible on the Bitcoin network within seconds of you hitting send, even though the transaction has not yet been written to the ledger. The other (non-mining) machines on the network make that happen. However, just like miners, these users have to update their software in order for new versions of Bitcoin to take hold. Just like miners, they can choose to run old or alternative versions of the software if they don't like what the developers have done.

End Users. Never underestimate the power of the end user. It is the people making transactions that give Bitcoin its value. No government, corporation, or other entity can put a gun to your head and force you to use a specific version of Bitcoin or to use Bitcoin at all. The end users can and will abandon any "new" version of Bitcoin that does not have their best interests at heart. This is the ultimate veto, and the developers and miners know it. Unfortunately, as the user base grows, the level of involvement of the average user is dropping. Most users don't care what the developers and miners are arguing about on a weekly basis... nor should they. The veto power of the end user will probably be wielded by the people who make the Bitcoin wallets, who can choose to implement or ignore changes to the protocol (within reason).

None of this implies that every change to Bitcoin is an epic struggle among these powerful parties. That isn't the case at all. Most changes to the Bitcoin protocol are minor, beneficial and noncontroversial. But when there are wildly different opinions on what effects a change might have, the process can be prolonged and extremely contentious. This is transparent to people just buying coffee with BTC, but investors and traders need to keep informed as part of their due diligence.

How Do I Get Bitcoin?

There are a lot of ways for a user to obtain bitcoin, but some are easier and more suitable for new users than others.

Online Bitcoin Exchanges.

The most straightforward way is to purchase them on an online exchange like Coinbase, or Kraken. These services will accept deposits of USD (usually from a bank account or credit card) and exchange those dollars for an equivalent amount of BTC. The process is easy, but there are a few things that new users should be aware of.

Online exchanges will request your personal information before they will work with you. You must provide a copy of a driver's license or similar ID and perhaps answer questions about the source of your funds. This is a federal requirement that anyone who has opened a bank or brokerage account should be familiar with. Those who are unfamiliar may consider this to be an invasion of privacy or balk at providing personal identifying information over the internet. Also note that the exchange may take time (minutes to days) to process the information you give them, and you will have restricted (or nonexistent) access to their services while they do so. In other words: Don't expect to open an account with an online exchange and immediately buy/sell massive amounts of BTC. You'll only end up frustrated. If you need to get your hands on some bitcoin immediately consider one of the other methods.

In the past, some online exchanges (I'm looking at you, Coinbase) have tracked the movement of the bitcoin that their customers bought. Recall that the Bitcoin ledger is public, and the exchange knows what address it sent the BTC to, making it trivial for them track its use for at least the first few transactions. Customers who used their newly purchased BTC to engage in illegal activity (on a gambling website, for instance) have had their accounts unexpectedly closed.

Online exchanges usually have a wallet associated with them. When you buy bitcoin, the BTC goes into your wallet at the exchange and stays there until you move it somewhere else. NEVER LEAVE YOUR BTC IN AN EXCHANGE'S WALLET! As soon as the purchase is complete, always move the BTC to a wallet you control. Always. The only exception is if you are engaged in day trading or arbitrage. New users shouldn't be doing either of those things. Why the emphasis on this point? Exchanges are not banks. In the short history of Bitcoin, exchanges have been hacked, have "lost" Bitcoin, have scammed users and gone bankrupt through their own incompetence. When an exchange is in trouble, one of the first things they do is block the withdrawal of BTC from their online wallets. Research an early Bitcoin exchange named "MtGox" for a stark lesson in why you NEVER leave money on an exchange.

Your bank may not like Bitcoin. There are documented cases of people who have had their transactions blocked or their accounts at major banks closed due to "suspicious activity" after sending money to an exchange. It didn't happen often and has not happened recently but it did happen.

When there is a sudden spike in demand, some exchanges cannot keep up. Their websites may become unavailable, or purchases and transactions may take a long time to complete. Unexplained cancellations of purchases are not unheard of.

In-Person exchange.

If you live in an area with a lot of Bitcoin users, you may be able to meet someone and conduct a cash dollar-to-BTC transaction. Services such as Localbitcoins (localbitcoins.com) and Mycelium Marketplace (via the Mycelium Wallet on Android) can connect buyers and sellers. This method is more private and potentially faster than using an exchange, but prices will be higher. There is also the matter of security. Conduct the transaction in a public, well-lit place, as you will be meeting an unknown person who knows you are carrying cash.

ATM

Yes, there are Bitcoin ATMs. No, there is probably not one near you. But they do exist, and you can use Google or CoinATMRadar to find one. CoinATMRadar also has an app you can load on your smartphone for mobile use. There are several types of ATM, and the exact procedure for using them varies. Be prepared to provide identification.

...And the rest

Some wallets like Mycelium have partnered with exchanges to provide the ability to buy and sell BTC from within the wallet itself, often using a credit/debit card. These are essentially just links to online exchanges. Expect to pay more for the convenience.

Services like BitQuick (www.bitquick.com) operate like a cross between Localbitcoins and a regular exchange. They connect buyers and sellers, but instead of meeting online, the exchange happens remotely, with the buyer depositing cash directly into the seller's bank account. There is usually some form of escrow involved to ensure no one gets cheated. Localbitcoins brokers this kind of service as well.

How NOT to obtain bitcoin

Bitcoin Faucets. These are websites that will send you very small amounts of BTC in exchange for you just visiting their page (which is full of advertisements). There is nothing wrong or illegal about faucets, but people new to Bitcoin tend to get the wrong idea about how much they can get this way. Faucets provide EXTREMELY small amounts (fractions of a cent), and you typically have to wait until you amass a minimum amount before they will send you your BTC. Unless you have a lot of patience and a high tolerance for frustration (and advertising) skip the faucets.

Scams, schemes, and "investments". Bitcoin's history is filled with schemes masquerading as "investments" that paid interest or dividends in BTC. Not all of them have been outright scams, but the vast majority were. Most of these were easy to identify as scams due to their wild claims of guaranteed results for little or no risk. Some made more believable claims yet still vanished suddenly or were shut down. If someone offers to pay you bitcoin dividends if you deposit your BTC with them or buy "stock" in their Bitcoin venture, run. Assume they are a scam, even if their numbers seem to add up. You will be right far more often than wrong.

Should I Invest In Bitcoin?

First, let's define some terms. By "invest," do you mean purchasing a large amount of BTC hoping you can sell it for a massive profit later (speculating)? Or do you mean buying and selling BTC to take profit from short-term price fluctuations (trading)?

If you mean either of these things, then:

Short Answer: Probably not.

Long Answer: This is not a book of investment advice. This is an introductory text who's intended audience is people who know little to nothing about Bitcoin. If there is one piece of investment wisdom I CAN provide, it is to not invest in things you do not understand. This book does not contain enough technical information for you to use as a basis for investment decisions.

Haven't people made a lot of money investing in Bitcoin?

Yes, they have. In early 2011, one BTC was worth $1 USD. Today, in 2017, one BTC is $2100. If you had invested in BTC when it was below one dollar, you would have amassed a life-changing amount of money in less than a decade. Plenty of people did. Some were developers or extremely knowledgeable hobbyists who saw the potential in Bitcoin and made a decision that turned out to be a mind-bogglingly profitable. Others were folks who heard about Bitcoin and, knowing little more about it beyond where to buy some, bought a bunch because other people were doing it. The first group of people was investors who knew what they were doing and took a calculated risk. The second group was gamblers who got lucky.

Both groups made money, right?

Sure. Bitcoin has made millionaires.

It also ruined people. The rise from cents to thousands of dollars was not a straight line. From late 2013 to early 2014, BTC experienced a drop from over $1200 to around $350. It did not return to the $1200 level until March of 2017. People who bought in at the top and sold in frustration when the price dropped lost a lot of money. At one point in 2014, the top post on the popular Bitcoin forum on Reddit was a link to a suicide hotline. **It was not a joke.**

If I may offer another piece of investment advice in addition to "Don't invest in things you don't understand," it would be "Do not invest money you can't afford to lose."

There are two things that must be true before you invest any significant amount of money into BTC: 1) You must be familiar with the technology at a level beyond what is presented in this book. 2) You must already be a successful investor or trader in commodities, stocks, or currencies.

If you are a new speculator or trader, Bitcoin is not a place for you to learn. If you are an experienced speculator or trader, you already know better than to jump into something blind.

For the record, I do not believe Bitcoin has exhausted its upward potential. There is still profit to be made in the long term, but only by those who tread carefully and put in the effort to learn what they're investing in. What I do recommend for Bitcoin newbies is learn the process of obtaining, spending, and securely storing Bitcoin by actually doing it yourself. Instead of money, invest time and energy. See how it works. See what problems Bitcoin solves and what problems it still has to overcome before it can achieve mass adoption. Participate in (or at least observe) discussions on places like Reddit or bitcointalk. It won't take long for you to appreciate Bitcoin's potential AND its weaknesses, enabling you to make investment decisions properly.

Is Bitcoin Secure?

Short Answer: Bitcoin is as secure as you and your computer are, but not one bit more.

Long Answer: True security can only be declared after a long history of successful resistance to attack. This is as true for currencies as it is for national borders or medieval castles. Bitcoin has been tested and attacked constantly since it first hit the internet in 2008. The Bitcoin network has survived these attacks and grown more resistant to them as developers fix bugs and address weaknesses. But is a track record of 9 years, or 19 years, or 29 years enough to declare anything "secure"? It depends...

Secure enough for what?

Any discussion of Bitcoin's security must begin with the question of use case. What do you use Bitcoin for? Most people are comfortable using bitcoin to purchase items online or in person. Bitcoin is "secure enough" for that use case, as the most you could lose in the event of an error or unforeseen problem is the equivalent of the cash in your pocket. But if you look at the opposite side of the transaction, the merchants, their exposure is much higher. A merchant may deal with thousands to tens of thousands of dollars in bitcoin. Would you be as comfortable with a $100,000 transaction in bitcoin as you are with a $1.00 one? What if your intent was to exchange BTC for USD after the transaction instead of holding the bitcoin in your wallet... does that make you more comfortable? How about storing your entire life savings in a Bitcoin address for 30 years? You must decide for yourself whether Bitcoin is "secure enough" for whatever you are trying to do. A large and growing number of people consider Bitcoin to be more secure than credit cards for online transactions. These same people would probably not be so cavalier about using it as long term storage for their entire net worth.

Secure against what?

What are the attacks you're expecting the Bitcoin network (and/or your wallet software) to protect you from? Hackers stealing your money? Someone using your personal information to ruin your credit? A software or network glitch that causes BTC to "vanish" from your wallet? A government or corporation blocking access to your funds? The list goes on, and includes many things that the average end user doesn't even consider, like inflation or fluctuations in exchange rates due to demand in other countries. Evaluating Bitcoin's security against every potential threat would be impossible, but you don't have to do that. You just need to decide which threats are your major concern.

Is it hackers stealing the money out of your wallet? While no software or network is 100% unbreakable, the nature of Bitcoin makes this unlikely. I hesitate to use the word "impossible", but I have zero concern about this threat. Explaining why would involve discussing encryption and other complex topics that I am intentionally avoiding in this text. Am I saying you should take Bitcoin's security on faith? No more than you take it on faith that the engine in your car won't catch fire when you turn the key. Note that I'm talking about the Bitcoin protocol here, NOT your computer or the specific wallet software you're using. Those I have a lot less faith in.

Perhaps theft isn't your concern, but the idea of a software glitch that "disappears" your money keeps you up at night. I am even less concerned about this than I am about hackers. Every Bitcoin transaction has a permanent record in a public, distributed ledger. A mistake in the Bitcoin protocol cannot change that ledger. A bug in your wallet software cannot go back in time and make your deposits disappear. Accomplishing that would require a tremendous amount of computing power that increases with every block of transactions written.

In 2012 the Republic of Cyprus underwent a serious financial crisis when it could no longer repay its debts. Cyprus' solution included temporarily freezing their citizens' access to money in banks, followed by a one-time levy on bank accounts with balances over a certain amount. In other words, they took money out of their citizens' bank accounts. This is not science fiction, ancient history or conspiracy theory; this actually happened less than a decade ago. This event caused many to become rightly concerned about it happening in other places. What would prevent it from happening in the US? What would stop the government from snatching away a portion of your hard-earned money? Bitcoin could stop it. Bitcoin that is in your wallet can only be accessed by you. Not the bank. Not the government. It is as secure from confiscation as cash (or gold or silver) in your pocket. The same cannot be said for funds in banks as the Cypriot people discovered in 2012.

What about price Volatility and Inflation? The value of a US Dollar (how much stuff it can buy) decreases over time due to inflation, but it does not change significantly from one day to the next. It is stable in the short term and trending downward in the long term. The value of bitcoin has experienced some exciting rises and drops in its history, some of which took place over days or weeks. The long term price trend, however, is upward. What does all this mean? It means that your bitcoin is 100% secure from inflation, but is very vulnerable to price volatility. Which one should you be worried about? Again, that depends on your use case. If you are using Bitcoin as a way to store money over the long term, then the lack of inflation and the upward price trend work in your favor. If you are using Bitcoin to buy and sell things, then both inflation and price volatility are irrelevant. Your time frame is probably too short for either of them to matter. If you are somewhere in between, however, things can get scary. If you are saving bitcoin for something you will need soon, but not right away, you might get bitten by some unexpected price volatility. Bitcoin is not a good way to store money for your vacation in a few months.

Are YOU secure?

One of the essential trade-offs of using Bitcoin is assuming full responsibility for securing your own wealth. There are a lot of people who can offer you advice and assistance, but the responsibility (and liability) is all on you. Remember those banks and payment processors that Bitcoin makes optional? Most credit cards do not hold you liable for charges if your account is compromised. If a bank folds and takes your money with it, FDIC insures you for up to $100,000. Neither of those is true for Bitcoin. If you remove the 3rd parties, you remove the protections (real or imagined) that they offer.

Are you ready for that responsibility?

Recall that bitcoin is stored in addresses, and you need a Bitcoin wallet to perform transactions with those addresses. The Bitcoin wallet is software that runs on your computer or your smartphone. Instead of (or in addition to) being concerned about whether Bitcoin is secure, you should ask yourself some questions about your own security:

Does your smartphone have a password?
Is it a GOOD password?
Do you ever install apps from sources other than the App Store or Play Store?
How strong is your computer's password?
Do you keep the operating system updated?
Do you keep the other software that you run updated?
Do you run cracked copies of games or software?
Does your computer have a virus or trojan?
How certain are you?
Are you certain enough to bet $100 on it?
How about $1000?
Or $10,000?

None of the above questions are specific to Bitcoin. People perform electronic banking functions on their phones and computers all the time, and the same cautions apply to them. The difference is that with banking, your bank will not hold you 100% accountable if a hacker uses your computer to empty your account. But Bitcoin isn't like a bank account. Bitcoin is like cash. No limited liability. No deposit insurance. If someone steals the cash out of your purse that cash is gone and you have no recourse for getting your money back aside from calling the police. If someone gets access to your Bitcoin wallet, your bitcoin becomes their bitcoin, and you are left in the unenviable position of trying to explain what a bitcoin is to the police. This does not mean that Bitcoin was hacked... it means that YOU were hacked. It wasn't Bitcoin's job to prevent that. It was yours.

Some are not ready for that level of responsibility for large (or any) fractions of their net worth. And that's okay. As a beginner, you should keep your use of Bitcoin at or below your comfort level until you are more educated in computer and Bitcoin security.

How can I be more secure in my use of Bitcoin?

Never re-use an address if you can avoid it. A Bitcoin address should only be used to receive funds once. When you wish to send more BTC to your wallet, send it to a new address in your wallet. (NOTE: An exception to this is cold or "paper" wallets, which I describe below.)

Set a passcode. Your phone and computer should have a passcode or password. If your Bitcoin wallet supports setting its own separate PIN number or passcode, do it. This makes it a little slower to access your BTC, but the extra security is worth it.

Back up your wallet. Your Bitcoin wallet is more than just a list of addresses. Each address has a unique secret code to access its contents. You'll probably never use those codes directly; the software handles that for you. Another thing the software should do is provide a way to back up those codes and restore them into a new wallet. The exact mechanism for doing this differs, but on smartphones, it usually involves the wallet showing you a long list of random words. Those words are the secret codes transformed into a format that is easier for humans to deal with. You don't need to memorize them. You need to write them down and keep them very, very secure. If your phone gets damaged or stolen, you can type those words into the wallet running on another phone and recover your bitcoin.

Do not leave BTC in an online wallet service, such as those offered by exchanges. Your Bitcoin wallet should be on your phone, on your computer, or on a special piece of hardware you've acquired for that purpose (see below). It should never be "in the cloud". If a website offers to keep your BTC for you, do NOT take them up on that offer. Even if the website is someone you trust with other things (such as an exchange where you buy BTC), letting anyone else control access to your BTC is a REALLY BAD IDEA. The only exception is traders who are buying/selling BTC for profit. In addition to losing money in a bad trade, one of the risks traders assume is that of losing money due to an exchange hack, malice or incompetence. Non-traders need not expose themselves to these risk. So don't.

Do not keep large sums of money in a computer or phone-based wallet. The definition of "large sum" varies with the individual, but you should treat a Bitcoin wallet like a physical wallet. If you don't walk around with your entire net worth in cash in your pocket, don't do it with Bitcoin. Instead, use hardware, paper, or offline wallets for large sums and/or long-term storage.

An offline wallet is a wallet on a machine which you leave offline and use for only one purpose: to store and transfer BTC. It is not used to surf the web. It is not used to play games. It is not used to check email. It is dedicated to Bitcoin and nothing else. Real-world examples may be an old smartphone or laptop you've wiped (factory reset), installed Bitcoin software on, and then disconnected from the internet. Even without a network connection, the addresses in these wallets can still receive bitcoin. You just can't make new transactions to spend the BTC without taking the machine online. Since the machine is not online, some virus or random hacker on the internet can't steal your bitcoin.

If you need something more secure and robust than an old phone, you can purchase a specialized piece of hardware such as a Trezor. This hardware wallet allows you to use any PC for BTC transactions, even if the PC is compromised. It is beyond the needs of a new user, but if you find yourself amassing a large quantity of BTC you may need to graduate to something like this. For now, just remember that these things exist.

My favorite method of offline storage is a paper wallet. A paper wallet is a piece of paper (or plastic or metal) with a Bitcoin address written on it, along with the secret code used to access the BTC. Recall from above that an address does not need to be online to receive bitcoin. You can send bitcoin to the address without fear that its associated computer will be hacked because there is no associated computer. In this way, it is similar to the offline wallets discussed above, but with no spare machine, to keep offline. When you need to spend the funds, most Bitcoin wallets will allow you to import the paper wallet address (using the secret code) and transfer its contents. This takes only a few seconds and is a lot less complicated than it sounds. I cannot overstate the need to protect the paper wallet from theft or destruction.

Also, obtaining a paper wallet is not as straightforward as using one. I do not recommend ordering them online, as you are trusting the creator not to record the secret codes before mailing them to you. There are websites like Bitaddress.org and walletgenerator.net that allow you to generate and print them yourself, but once again you are trusting the website not to secretly record the codes. The proper method is to download the creation software yourself, run it on your PC and print the resulting addresses and codes to a printer physically connected to your computer. As with hardware wallets, a paper wallet is not something a new user needs to worry about; just remember they are an option.

Do NOT use a Brain Wallet. A brain wallet is a paper wallet without the paper. The secret codes I've mentioned above are long strings of random letters and numbers impossible for the average person to remember or guess. But what if you COULD remember one? In that case, you would have a Bitcoin address you could access by typing the random gibberish into some wallet software. So now what if someone made a Bitcoin address who's secret code was something easy to remember? Then they would have a brain wallet. Unfortunately, things that are easy to remember (like quotes, song lyrics, or passages from books) are also easy for computers to guess. If you created a brain wallet with an easy-to-remember secret code and sent BTC to it, there is a near 100% chance that someone has ALREADY guessed it and imported it into their wallet. Their computers are now watching YOUR address, waiting to steal whatever money you send to it.

Is Bitcoin Anonymous?

Short answer: No. However, with sufficient effort, you can make it extremely difficult to tie your Bitcoin transactions to your identity. Note that "extremely difficult" and "impossible" are **_not_** the same thing.

Long Answer: The public ledger contains a record of every Bitcoin transaction. The ledger is viewable by anyone. However, recall that the ledger doesn't contain names or identifying information associated with the transactions. All you will see are addresses, timestamps, and amounts. Specifically, you will see the addresses from which the bitcoins in the transaction originated (sources) and the addresses where they were sent (destinations). If you looked at one of those source or destination addresses you will see more transactions with still more addresses. You can trace the bitcoin forward and backward in time to either their current address or the address where they were generated.

But if none of this information contains a name, address, or social security number, doesn't that mean everything is anonymous? No. A sufficiently motivated person can discover enough trace information to unmask your identity and/or the identities of those you transact with. If at any point your bitcoins touch an entity that knows your real-world identity (such as an employer or a Bitcoin exchange), then your identity can be divulged with a subpoena (or other means), and then your transactions can be traced across the ledger with your name now attached to them.

So how does one go about making their identity harder to obtain? The simplest way is to never use the same Bitcoin address twice. Instead, use your wallet software to generate a new recipient address for every transaction in which you are receiving BTC.

You can also avoid buying or selling Bitcoin on an exchange, and instead purchase your BTC with in-person transactions.

If someone wanted to take their privacy to the next level, they can use a mixer or tumbler service to obfuscate the source of their bitcoin. Tumblers create a series of transactions among multiple users. At the end, each user gets back the same amount of BTC that they put in (minus fees) but they do not receive the exact same coins. Picture it this way: Suppose someone had recorded the serial numbers of all the dollar bills you own to track your spending. You and three strangers put all the cash you have into a cardboard box. You shake the box and then withdraw the same amount of cash you dropped in. You have just as much money as you had before, but you (hopefully) don't have the exact same bills. Whoever was tracking you would have to find a way to associate your identity with your NEW dollar bills, as the old association is no longer valid.

Don't worry if this sounds complicated or unnecessary. Tumbling and mixing can be confusing, and most new Bitcoin users shouldn't concern themselves with tumbling beyond the knowledge that such services exist.

What Challenges Does Bitcoin Face?

The Bitcoin community tends to view Bitcoin's longevity as a foregone conclusion. Bitcoin's success, however, is not assured. There are obstacles that Bitcoin has to overcome before it can go mainstream:

Capacity. Under the current architecture, Bitcoin has a limited capacity for the number of transactions it can handle per hour. Recall that transactions are written to the public ledger in blocks, and a block is written every 10 minutes on average. There is also a limit on the size of a block. This restricts the number of transactions that the network can handle per hour. This was not a problem when Bitcoin was small and relatively unknown, but as Bitcoin moved out of the realm of hobbyists and into the mainstream, the system's capacity became a growth-limiting obstacle that still needs to be addressed.

The Bitcoin community is undergoing a vigorous debate on just how to do so. Some want to increase the maximum size of the blocks. Some want to alter the way the protocol functions so that transactions can be smaller and more of them can fit into blocks. Still others want to take no action and let the free market (or "fee market" in this case) do its job. The details of these potential solutions are beyond this introductory text, but until some solution is reached, users should expect increasing fees and/or longer wait times as the backlog of unwritten transactions grows.

Increasing Fees. One of the original selling points of Bitcoin was the low cost of transferring funds, regardless of distance or amount. This is still a valuable part of Bitcoin's allure. However, the fees required to transact in BTC have risen considerably. Years ago it may have cost one cent to send a transaction. Today that same transaction may cost you $1.15. While the transaction fees are still much lower than competing traditional systems such as Western Union, they eat away at Bitcoin's suitability for sending small amounts or buying low-cost items. After all, why would someone spend $1 to send $2.50 to someone? Some of the upward pressure on fees will dissipate when a solution to capacity limit is implemented. But fee increase due to exchange rate will continue as long as bitcoin increases in value, which may be for quite a while.

Merchant Acceptance. The number of merchants that accept BTC is still a small percentage of those that accept traditional payment methods like credit cards. However, there has been tremendous growth in recent years, and that growth does not appear to be slowing. Also, companies like Gyft (which allows you to use bitcoin to purchase gift cards) and Purse.io (where you can purchase items from Amazon with bitcoin) help bridge the ever-shrinking gap. The limited acceptance of Bitcoin is a problem that has been shrinking for some time and will continue to do so.

Public Perception. Bitcoin has been accused of being a Ponzi scheme, being a tool of terrorists, drug dealers and/or pedophiles, being 'dead' or otherwise doomed to imminent failure, being a government conspiracy... the list goes on. And yet Bitcoin continues to not only exist but prosper. But that doesn't mean that Bitcoin is bulletproof. People resist change, and Bitcoin represents a massive change in the financial industry. It is not just a tool that could make the current financial infrastructure more efficient, it can make large parts of that infrastructure irrelevant. To say a certain amount of resistance and name-calling should be expected is an understatement. People tend not to like things they don't understand, and Bitcoin is very complex. The community of developers, enthusiasts, and entrepreneurs that have brought Bitcoin from the hobbyist fringe to the verge of mainstream acceptance must continue to push public awareness and positive perception. And they must do this without sounding like rabid cultists or sleazy scam artists. If they fail, Bitcoin fails. The phrase "perception is reality" is not meant to be taken literally; it means that people tend to react to their perceptions as if they were real, regardless of whether they are or not. Applied to Bitcoin, this truism means that if the public views Bitcoin as a terrorist pedophile scam-currency, they will not only abandon it, but insist upon its extermination. And unlike other currencies, Bitcoin does not have a government fiat to force people to continue using it. Public perception is a vulnerability that should not be ignored.

Regulatory Pressures. When Bitcoin became popular, governments didn't know how to react. They had the same questions and preconceived notions that people have today: What exactly is Bitcoin? Is it a scam? Is it anonymous? They also had additional questions of "How do we tax it?" and "How can we find people who are using it for illegal activity?" For the most part, the US Government took a hands-off approach similar to the one they took with the internet as a whole. Laws needed to be obeyed and taxes needed to be paid as with anything else, but regulating Bitcoin itself was not on their agenda. Some state governments took a more heavy-handed approach. New York, for instance, made it mandatory that Bitcoin companies go through the arduous process of getting a money transmitter license before conducting business. Several companies either shut down or relocated because of that law. Since then, several other states have enacted similar requirements, thus impeding the grown of the Bitcoin economy while (arguably) protecting users. The good news is that the actual use of Bitcoin by end-users is unaffected by these laws. Federal and State tax law still treats BTC as a commodity, forcing users to calculate capital gains on every transaction. Regardless of whether you agree with regulation (and there are many in the Bitcoin community that do) the real problem here is uncertainty. Governments on any level can change their minds about Bitcoin's legality and their regulatory stance toward it at any time. Russia, for instance, banned Bitcoin altogether. Then they decided to un-ban it. This problem, however, is not unique to Bitcoin. It is shared by any technology from firearms to encryption.

Complexity. Bitcoin is complicated. It will not get any less complicated as time goes by. Well-designed software with simple user interfaces can mask this complexity from end users, but there will always be a learning curve. While mobile Bitcoin wallets are simple enough to be used by almost anyone, desktop wallets still have a way to go. Also, the common-sense rules of using Bitcoin are not yet common. When someone falls into this gap by, for example, sending a transaction without a fee, it is not clear what happens or where they can turn for help. This needs to change. Bitcoin may never be as easy to use as cash, but it can be every bit as simple (and more secure) than a credit card. Eventually.

Keeping It Simple

This book has thrown a lot of new concepts and information at you. If you found it hard to keep track of it all, here are the essential ideas of this book. This is what you need to remember:

1. Bitcoin is like cash for the internet.
2. The word "bitcoin" can refer to the Bitcoin network, the Bitcoin software, or the bitcoin currency (BTC).
3. Bitcoin is not a scam.
4. Bitcoin is legal.
5. Bitcoin transactions are irreversible.
6. Bitcoin is not anonymous.
7. Bitcoin is not free to use, despite what some people might tell you.
8. You can purchase bitcoin on exchanges that are required to collect your personal details.
9. NEVER LEAVE PURCHASED BITCOIN ON AN EXCHANGE
10. Mining Bitcoin is expensive and not for beginners.
11. Speculating or trading in Bitcoin is also not for beginners.
12. Don't invest in things you don't understand.

13. Don't risk money you can't afford to loose.
14. NEVER LEAVE PURCHASED BITCOIN ON AN EXCHANGE
15. Bitcoin is as secure as you are... but no more.
16. The weak point in Bitcoin security is your computer or smartphone, not Bitcoin itself.
17. The safest way to store BTC long-term is in a paper wallet, hardware wallet, or other offline wallet.
18. NEVER LEAVE PURCHASED BITCOIN ON AN EXCHANGE. (Don't say you weren't warned).

"How do I get started?" and *"How to I buy bitcoin?"* are asked so often that the book wouldn't be complete without attempting to address those questions. Here is a simplified list of steps to get started with Bitcoin:

1. Put a passcode/password on your phone or desktop if you don't already have one.
2. Decide on a wallet. Consider Mycelium (Android) or Breadwallet (iOS). Both are free.
3. Install the wallet and follow the instructions to back up your wallet. This will probably involve writing down and re-entering random words.
4. Go back and follow the instructions to back up your wallet. Do it.
5. Register at an exchange. There are many. If you don't have time to research for yourself, just use Coinbase or Kraken... flip a coin.
6. Satisfy the exchange's KYC ("Know Your Customer") requirements, which may include you sending them a picture of your driver's license.
7. Use the exchange to purchase BTC with either a bank account or credit card.
8. Transfer your BTC to your wallet.
9. DO NOT SKIP THE PREVIOUS STEP.

Congratulations, you now own bitcoin. Obviously, the detailed instructions for many of the above steps will depend on the exact wallet and exchange you are using. Exchanges will gladly answer questions and help new users if asked.

Where Can I Learn More?

You've reached the end of the book. You now know the basics of Bitcoin and know what all the "fuss" is about. The obvious question is how can you learn more. The web is full of helpful people who love to teach and talk about Bitcoin. I recommend the following:

R/Bitcoinbeginners
A Reddit forum dedicated to helping beginners. This is where you can go to ask questions.
https://www.reddit.com/r/BitcoinBeginners/

Introduction to Bitcoin
An excellent introductory video from one of the best minds in Bitcoin, Andreas Antonopoulos.
https://www.youtube.com/watch?v=l1si5ZWLgy0

Bitcoin Whitepaper
This is the official document that defines the Bitcoin protocol. Parts of it are fairly technical.
https://bitcoin.org/bitcoin.pdf

Let's Talk Bitcoin
A hub of podcasts and articles dedicated to Bitcoin. There is almost too much information here for one person to consume.

https://letstalkbitcoin.com/

Understanding Bitcoin:

A Beginner's Guide To Cryptocurrency

By

Eric Morse

To the early adopters, who learned all of this the hard way so that others wouldn't have to.

Table of Contents

Introduction

Bitcoin is quite popular lately, and rightfully so. This new technology provides people the world over with an alternative way to shop, save, invest, and transact outside of the traditional financial infrastructure. In the Philippines, for example, when one of the country's biggest banks went offline for two days in June of 2017, millions were unable to pay their bills and daily expenses. But a few had already embraced Bitcoin and were able to pay for many of the things they needed those two days. In 2010, traditional payment processors (Visa, MasterCard and Paypal) stopped doing business with Wikileaks, completely disabling that organization's ability to collect donations. Enter: Bitcoin. Wikileaks funded itself almost exclusively through Bitcoin for some time, and Bitcoin still has a prominent place on their donations page.

In this book, you'll learn what Bitcoin is and how to use it securely to pay for goods and services. I'll also touch on using Bitcoin as an alternative form of investment, and how to invest should you decide to do so. By the end, you'll be in a good position to start using Bitcoin for practical and investment purposes.

This book assumes that you have not read any of my previous works on cryptocurrency. Out of necessity, it will cover some of the same ground as <u>Bitcoin: A Simple Introduction</u>, which focused on presenting the basics of Bitcoin in the most simple way possible. That book shied away from certain topics (mining and investing, for example) that I didn't see as suitable for an intro-level primer. With only a few exceptions it also didn't name specific websites, software or businesses. Those blinders are removed for this book. *Understanding Bitcoin* is intended for the slightly more advanced beginner, if there is such a thing. It is for people who want to know **"Where To Go"** and **"What To Do,"** whereas *A Simple Introduction* is more focused on **"What is This Bitcoin Thing I Keep Hearing About?"**.

Some things to know up front:

Things change rapidly on the internet and change even faster in the world of Bitcoin. If you are reading this book years after I've written it (in early 2017) the companies and websites I discuss in this book may have gone out of business or significantly changed their areas or methods of operation.

Also, the Bitcoin ecosystem is large and growing. Since this book is not a directory of Bitcoin businesses, I cannot list every business, website, hardware vendor, etc. I chose to list those that are the most well-known or that I have had personal experience with in the past. If I do not mention a specific business or website, it should not be taken as a warning, negative opinion, or statement of disapproval. With the exception of links to my other books, I have not included any affiliate links in this text. I do not have a financial stake in any business or product mentioned.

Finally, while Bitcoin is global, companies and regulations are not. While I do discuss other countries, this book is mostly intended for an American audience. Therefore, unless I specifically mention another country, you should assume I'm speaking about the US.

If you're ready and excited to learn about Bitcoin, turn the page so we can get started.

Chapter One: SuperMoney

Bitcoin is the first, most popular, and most successful of the cryptocurrencies.

But what exactly does that mean?

Cryptocurrencies are money on steroids. They are the digital equivalent of (and competitor to) more familiar currencies like Dollars, Euros, etc. They use technology and cryptography to provide users with capabilities beyond what can be done with with the monetary and payment systems they're accustomed to. Cryptocurrencies are to money what superheroes are to regular people.

So how exactly are they better?

Cryptocurrencies are bulletproof. By that, I mean they are resistant to interference by third parties. Bitcoin transactions operate like cash over the internet. Once the transaction is confirmed, the BTC is *yours*... 100% resistant to banks, payment processors, lawyers, politicians, or men with guns who may want to meddle with the transaction without your permission. Your funds are as secure as money in your pocket... something that is demonstrably untrue with credit cards and Paypal.

Cryptocurrencies are unstoppable. No one can stop you from doing business with another person using a cryptocurrency such as Bitcoin. The same is true for cash... but you can't use cash over the internet. The introduction to this book mentioned two examples (Wikileaks and BPI) where some entity stood in the way of people conducting transactions with one another. Bitcoin makes such interference impossible. Shutting down Bitcoin would require shutting down the internet as a whole.

Cryptocurrencies are fast. People who've used Bitcoin may be raising their hands to object here. After all, a Bitcoin transaction make minutes to hours to confirm, while a credit card transaction goes through in seconds. But that's not exactly a fair comparison. When you buy something with a credit or debit card, that transaction is approved in seconds... but money doesn't actually change hands (from the credit card company to the merchant) until several days after the purchase. This delay is invisible to the purchaser, making it seem like everything happened in the blink of an eye while the merchant only has the promise of money to be received days later. Cryptocurrencies like Bitcoin don't hide that delay... but the delay is only a few minutes or hours vs several days. For a purchaser this is no big deal. But the merchant standing across the counter from them has suddenly started paying attention.

Cryptocurrencies are intelligent. Cryptocurrencies have scripting capabilities that enable them to do things that cash cannot, such as multi-key transactions that require multiple people to spend from an account, or payment channels that allow frequent transactions among parties without each transaction being recorded to the ledger. Someone just using cryptocurrency to make purchases or send money overseas may not be interested in these more esoteric superpowers, but the ability to create "rules" under which money must be spent is a big deal to businesses, banks, and other financial entities that have been eying blockchain technology (i.e. cryptocurrencies) for some time.

There are more, of course, and not all cryptocurrencies are equally strong in each area. That's the whole point. One of the distinguishing features of Bitcoin spin-off Litecoin is its shorter transaction time. Litecoin is faster. One of the main differences between Ethereum and Bitcoin is that Ethereum has a more robust scripting language... it is "smarter". But Bitcoin is the original, most valuable, and most popular. If cryptocurrencies were superheroes... Bitcoin would be Superman.

How it Works

While conventional currencies are backed up by financial or government institutions, cryptocurrencies are backed by one of the most favorite subjects of students the world over: math. Cryptocurrencies use a dispersed network of computers that allows for what's called a peer-to-peer (P2P) method of transacting. A P2P system is one that doesn't require the services of a middleman or an agent. With Bitcoin and most other cryptocurrencies, this P2P system makes use of a public distributed ledger (blockchain) and mathematical algorithms (encryption and hashing) to maintain security and the integrity of the ledger.

Each account ("Bitcoin address") has an associated secret code ("private key") that the system uses to assert that address's control over the bitcoin the address contains. When bitcoin is spent, the address must provide its private key. Fortunately, most end users don't work with the keys directly and will probably never see one. The wallet software and the Bitcoin network handles all that for them.

Each Bitcoin transaction is simply a record of how currency has moved from a set of source addresses to a set of destination addresses. The Bitcoin protocol performs a number of actions... verifying that the source addresses actually controls the BTC being moved, for instance... and then writes the transaction to the blockchain.

Special Bitcoin users called "miners" are responsible for writing the transactions. This isn't as simple or straightforward as it sounds. Each miner or group (pool) of miners is constantly working on a specific mathematical problem. Not only is this problem difficult, it actually becomes MORE difficult as more people try to solve it. The first to solve the problem correctly gets to write the next block of transactions to the ledger. In return for their effort, they earn some newly created bitcoin, plus they get to keep all the transaction fees in the block they just wrote. In the case of a mining pool, this reward is distributed to the members in the pool, usually based on the amount of work each member contributed. The miner that writes the block gets to pick which transactions get written... and it's in their best interest to pick the transactions that have transaction fees associated with them. Thus, while the transaction fees are technically optional, if you want the miners to care enough about your transaction to write it, you should always include the appropriate fee. All of this applies to Bitcoin, but most other cryptocurrencies operate similarly, with differences in the exact math problem being solved, how the difficulty scales, how miners are rewarded, etc.

Most, but not all, cryptocurrencies have a cap on their maximum number of currency units. For Bitcoin, this is 21 million. Other altcoins have higher, lower, or no cap at all. The mining process above introduces new bitcoin slowly over time until the cap is reached. This process is much more controlled, gradual, and predictable than fiat currencies, which have no cap and no limit to their rate of increase.

Chapter Two: Power and Responsibility

Bitcoin was created by Satoshi Nakamoto (a pseudonym) in 2008. His intention was to give the world a digital currency with no central governing or controlling body, and resistance to interference from 3rd parties like banks, payment processors, and, yes... governments. Within this system, every user is their own bank. Every user has 100% control over their money. But along with this power comes some heightened responsibilities.

Autonomy

With Bitcoin you don't need anyone's consent or permission to spend your money. Not your parent's, not your government's, not your bank's. Unlike traditional bank accounts that your government can "freeze" or hold, your Bitcoin wallets are impervious to such actions by monetary authorities.

The Bitcoin autonomy doesn't end with just the financial transactions. It also extends to your privacy. With credit card companies, you are required to divulge your personal information if you want to use their payment system. But not Bitcoin, which allows you to keep your privacy intact. To be clear... you will probably need to identify yourself to an exchange when you purchase bitcoin, but after that initial purchase the movement of BTC among people is free of personally identifying information. You don't need to give your name and address to a vendor to buy something (unless, of course, they're shipping something to you). Every time you hear about a major retailer getting hacked and their customer's payment data being released, remember that with Bitcoin, there was no need for them to even have that data.

Because Bitcoin is a decentralized monetary system, geographic or legal restrictions won't prevent you from doing business with whoever you want, whenever you want, for whatever you want. This doesn't mean that Bitcoin makes illegal things legal... it means that it's up to YOU to obey the law.

Unique Transactional Features of Bitcoin

Bitcoin has unique features that set it apart from the traditional, centralized monetary systems people are used to. One of them is irreversibility. Once your transaction is written to the blockchain it cannot be canceled, reversed or modified. That's why, when transacting with bitcoin, you must ensure accuracy and security. Bitcoin is like cash in this respect. If you give someone a twenty dollar bill instead of a five and don't realize it until later, you are most likely out of luck. There's no way to "reverse" the cash payment and fix the error. Ditto for Bitcoin.

Another transactional feature is pseudo-anonymity. Bitcoin addresses are random chains of about 30 characters. Your addresses and transactions are innately tied your real-world identity. There is some ambiguity in that last sentence, so let's clarify with some examples:

If you buy something from an online store that needs to be shipped to you, the vendor knows your name and physical address. They also know your Bitcoin address, and can easily connect one with the other. The same is true of exchanges where you buy your bitcoin. They know who you really are and what address they sent bitcoin to. But this connection isn't part of the Bitcoin protocol, it exists outside of it... it comes from the need of the vendor to mail you something, and the legal requirement of the exchange to verify your identity.

You may remember me defining the Bitcoin blockchain as public distributed ledger. Did you catch the word 'public' in that description? It means exactly what you think: your transactions are visible to anyone who cares to look. Total strangers. Your nosy neighbor. The IRS. Anyone. What they'll see is bitcoins moving between addresses. They won't see names, social security numbers, or the fact that you bought condoms at the corner market last night. They won't know which addresses are yours unless you've told them or you've been careless in your use of Bitcoin. Your transactions can be analyzed and traced, but exposing your real identity is quite difficult, and can be made more difficult with some simple steps that I'll talk about in a later chapter.

Another key transactional feature of Bitcoin is security. Your bitcoin can only be accessed by a person who knows the private key of your account, which is you! Technically, your private keys are in your Bitcoin wallet. The wallet should have a password. The phone or computer holding your wallet should be secure. It's up to you to make those things happen. Remember: you are the bank. Powerful cryptography makes it much harder to hack your Bitcoin account compared to traditional bank or credit card accounts.... But if you have a bad password, all that encryption is powerless. The most powerful deadbolt in the world is no good if the door is rotten or the lock isn't fully engaged. However, if you take your duties as the "Bank of Your Own Money" seriously, you gain a truly amazing power: Bulletproof Finances.

Potential Challenges

While Bitcoin offers substantial advantages, it also has its share of challenges. Many of them are not vulnerabilities of Bitcoin itself, but rather of associated businesses, technologies, or people whose weaknesses or actions reflect badly on cryptocurrency as a whole.

Scams and Hacks are a perfect example of this. As soon as bitcoin obtained a monetary value, people began trying to take it from others through theft or fraud. Because Bitcoin is new, some users are unaccustomed to treating it as real money... even though it is. As a result, they fall victim to schemes and scams that they would never fall for if they were dealing with dollars or Euros. Here are some common examples:

Cloud Mining Scams: These are schemes where fictitious companies will propose mining bitcoin on your behalf in exchange for a substantial payment. After paying them, they'll disappear with your money. Note: cloud mining is not ITSELF a scam. There are legitimate cloud mining companies... but if you are new to Bitcoin you should probably avoid them as well. Cloud mining contracts are generally not worth it.

Online Wallets: Here, a company asks you to trust them with your private keys. Instead of using a wallet that YOU control, you use one that THEY control. And then the online wallet gets hacked. Sometimes the "hack" may be a ruse, and the wallet operator has run off with your bitcoin. Millions of dollars have disappeared just like this.

Exchange Scams/Hacks: Exchanges are where you buy/sell bitcoin and other cryptocurrencies. An exchange that is an outright fake is rare... but certainly possible. What you'll most likely see is a legitimate exchange that is careless with their security and gets hacked. Exchanges are like stealth online wallets. When you buy bitcoin, your purchase is stored on the exchange in a wallet that they control. Remember the previous paragraph about Online Wallets? The same applies here. The problem is most people don't realize or consider the exchange to be a wallet... and some exchanges actually encourage you to use their wallet. Don't. Exchanges are for buying... not storing or transacting.

Ponzi Schemes: These are typically ultra-high yield investment schemes that offer you outrageously high and guaranteed yields on your Bitcoin investments. The red flags here are the words "high" and "guaranteed" because the cardinal law in all investments is that the higher your expected return or yield, the higher the risk you must be willing to take. There's no such thing as zero-risk investment that offers yields or returns that are much better than what traditional investments can offer.

The complexity of Bitcoin is another challenge. For the first few years after Bitcoin's release it was not suitable for the general public... regardless of what some claimed. It was difficult to use, and doing so securely required an understanding of concepts like encryption that most people don't have. The situation is much better now. Bitcoin is easier to used than a credit card in most cases . Problem solved? Not quite. If there is a problem in your transaction... if you forget to include a fee, for instance... it is not clear where to get help, and sometimes the advice received is indecipherable to new users. In other words, Bitcoin is only easy on the surface, where most people will normally operate. But that veneer of simplicity is very thin. If someone has to pull back the curtain for any reason, the full complexity may overwhelm them. This isn't acceptable for some people. Bitcoin needs to be simple even when things don't work right... not just when they do.

The volatility of Bitcoin is another hurdle that keeps many from using or continuing to use it. Because many people are risk averse, they either shy away from or stop using bitcoin after experiencing significant "paper" loss due to the swings in the exchange rate. To be clear: all currencies have swings in value. Bitcoin just has and larger, more frequent ones. For some, this volatility is a problem. Others, however, see opportunities to invest.

Lastly, the increasing popularity of Bitcoin has led to increases in the fees required to validate transactions in a reasonable amount of time. This is an issue with scalability. On average, a block of transactions is written to the blockchain every ten minutes. But a block has a size limit. It can only hold a finite number of transactions, and miners will chose to include transactions with higher fees. This can lead to some transactions languishing in a backlog while several blocks go by without them. There are several technological solutions being considered to solve this problem, from simply increasing the block size limit to changing the protocol so that transactions are smaller, and so on. The debate over these solutions has been contentious, but it is clear that something must be done quickly if Bitcoin is to scale beyond its current size.

Chapter Three: Obtaining Bitcoin

There are a number of ways to obtain bitcoin. Buying BTC on an exchange is as straightforward as exchanging dollars for euros, gold, or anything else. However, Bitcoin's digital nature has given it an aura of mystery. People seek answers on how to obtain Bitcoin as if doing so were some epic quest involving digital sacrifices in secret corners of the internet, all of which must be kept from the all-seeing eyes of the law. None of that is true.

So here, in the most straightforward language possible, are several ways you can get your hands on some bitcoin. As you'll see, there are no secrets or arcane mysteries involved.

Using Exchanges

You can buy bitcoin online using your local currency through exchanges. There are dozens of them, but if you are new to Bitcoin, you should probably stick with the more well-known exchanges.

If you are a resident of the United States, Coinbase (www.coinbase.com) and Kraken (www.kraken.com) are two of the more popular Bitcoin exchanges. You typically pay using credit cards or bank transfers. If you are from the United Kingdom, Bittylicious (bittylicious.com) is a good way to buy your bitcoin, with the caveat that they only do business in the United Kingdom. If you are looking for an exchange that works in different countries within the European Union, Bitstamp (www.bitstamp.com) may be a better alternative for you.

If you live in Australia your best bet would be CoinJar (www.coinjar.com). In neighboring New Zealand, you can visit BitPrime (www.bitprime.co.nz) to get your bitcoin. While it's still a relatively young Bitcoin exchange, it works well with most New Zealand bank accounts.

In China, try OKCoin (www.okcoin.cn) and BTCC (www.btcchina.com), the first and second largest exchanges in that country, respectively.

In India, Unocoin (www.unocoin.com) and Zebpay (www.zebpay.com) are worth checking out.

For other parts of the world, use the search function at BuyBitcoinWorldwide (www.buybitcoinworldwide.com) to find an exchange in your country.

And if you are looking for a way to buy Bitcoins outside of organized exchanges, you can try LocalBitcoins.com, which supports cash, wire transfer, credit card, and PayPal for Bitcoin purchases. LocalBitcoins isn't technically an exchange. Rather than sell BTC to you directly in exchange for dollars, this website facilitates peer-to-peer and sometimes face-to-face exchanges among Bitcoin users. You use the LocalBitcoins website to find someone who is willing to exchange currencies with you directly. Since you're dealing with people you don't know, LocalBitcoins.com offers a risk mitigation system in the form of an escrow service. Use it.

You can also buy bitcoin using other cryptocurrencies or altcoins. Once again, you'll be using an exchange to perform this transaction. The difference is that the exchange might not accept USD or other fiat currencies as payment. You'll need to deposit some other cryptocurrency such as Litecoin or Ether. Examples of this type of exchange include Bittrex (www.bittrex.com) and Shapeshift.io (www.shapeshift.io).

You can also buy bitcoin through local ATMs where legal and available. You can use Coinatmradar.com to locate ATMs where you can buy bitcoin at a location near you. Such ATMs are also referred to as BTMs or Bitcoin Teller Machines.

If you prefer, you can also buy bitcoin in an entirely offline, face-to-face transaction through local Bitcoin meetups. Visit www.meetup.com/topics/bitcoin/all/ and bitcoin.xyz/meetup/ to find one near you.

Earning Bitcoin

You're not limited to merely exchanging one currency for another; you can also obtain bitcoin in exchange for your time, energy and talents. If it sounds like I'm talking about a job, you're almost right. While it is certainly possible to find a full-time job that pays you in bitcoin, such jobs aren't plentiful and this isn't a book on job-hunting. Instead, let's explore some more generally useful options.

Jobs4Bitcoin (www.reddit.com/r/Jobs4Bitcoins/) is a subreddit dedicated to connecting people who want things done with people who want bitcoin for doing things. If you have talent or experience in writing, programming, graphic design, translating, or any number of other areas, you can browse the listings to see if anyone is hiring. Or you can make a post of your own announcing your availability for paying gigs. Be prepared to provide samples of your work.

If you are looking for something a little more structured than a Reddit forum, try Xbtfreelancer (www.xbtfreelancer.com) or Bitgigs (bitgigs.com), which both offer similar services.

Do you have a website that gets a decent amount of traffic? There are numerous bitcoin advertising networks that operate similar to Google Adsense, where you "rent out" portions of your site to online advertisers. Note that your site has to be very popular before you can earn more than a few dollars worth of bitcoin per month. If you're interested check out Anonymous Ads (www.a-ads.com).

Avoid so-called "Bitcoin faucets," which pay you trivial amounts of bitcoin in exchange for viewing web pages. I have yet to see one of these that paid a decent return for your time. Not only do they not pay well, but they use increasingly frustrating "anti-cheat" mechanisms that will raise your blood pressure while you earn those tiny fractions of a cent.

Mining Bitcoin

Recall from a previous chapter that Bitcoin transactions are written to the blockchain by miners. The Bitcoin protocol rewards miners with the fees included in the transactions, and with a "block reward" of 12.5 BTC for each block of transactions. The block reward is how new bitcoin gets added to the economy. Since there is a cap of 21 million BTC, the block reward goes down every few years and will eventually vanish altogether when the cap is reached. Also recall that the Bitcoin protocol makes mining more difficult as more people participate.

The idea of creating money out of thin air with your computer was very attractive to Bitcoin early adopters. So much so that the mining difficulty quickly increased beyond the ability of normal computer hardware to keep up. People used to be able to mine profitably with their desktops or laptops. Within a few years only powerful gaming PCs with expensive graphics cards could turn a profit. Shortly after that, companies started producing specialized hardware that outperformed even these powerful gaming PCs. Then the race was on. Specialized mining hardware has gotten more powerful and more expensive every year... for years.

Because of the increasing requirements and costs of mining, miners have come together to create large "pools." These mining pools combine their individual mining power (or "hashrate"). The resulting bitcoin is shared among members of the pool. This idea suffered from the same fate as solo mining. Even as a group, advances in technology made mining unprofitable for people lacking specialized hardware.

I want to be clear here: Bitcoin mining is still profitable. But not without an up-front investment in specialized mining hardware and a source of cheap (or free) electricity to run and cool that hardware. So, while it is still technically possible to mine bitcoin with whatever PC you have on your desk, the current level of competition and the resulting difficulty make this a waste of time and electricity. Don't bother.

If you are still determined to make some of this "magic internet money" the hard (and expensive) way, here's what you'll need to do:

First you'll need to buy some hardware. The actual purchase should be done last, but you need to take a look at what's available and get a feel for how much mining power you can afford to buy. Bitmain has been producing specialized Bitcoin mining hardware for quite some time, but there are other vendors as well. There is a list of Bitmain's products at shop.bitmain.com/main.htm. When you visit, you need to look at more than just the price. You need to note the hashrates, usually given in mega-hashes per second (MH/s) or tera-hashes per second (TH/s), and the power consumption. You'll also need to pay attention to the availability dates, as their website lists items that are not yet in production. Write all of this information down for the unit(s) you can afford, but do not buy anything yet.

Next, you'll need to figure out how much your electricity costs. Bitcoin miners run on electricity. The more powerful the hardware, the higher it will drive your electric bill. This isn't a cost you can ignore. Look at your utility bill and figure out your cost in dollars per kilowatt/hour.

Now find the current network hashrate and mining difficulty from a site like BitcoinWisdom (bitcoinwisdom.com/bitcoin/difficulty). These may or may not be necessary for the next step, but they are crucial to your long term profitability. You should know what they mean and how to find the current values.

Since you probably won't be solo mining, find a mining pool. AntPool (www.antpool.com) is a very large, very popular pool, but you should investigate others. Use the mining pool list at Bitcoin Wiki (en.bitcoin.it/wiki/Comparison_of_mining_pools). You'll quickly discover there is more to mining pools than you first imagined. For now, take note of any fees that participants have to pay, and whether the pool distributes transaction fees to participants. Learning about "merged mining", "reward types", etc. is homework that you can save until later... just don't actually start mining until you know what these mean.

Next, visit a mining calculator such as Cryptocompare (www.cryptocompare.com/mining/calculator/) or 99Bitcoins (99bitcoins.com/bitcoin-mining-calculator/). At a minimum, you'll need to enter the hardware price, power consumption, hashrate and electricity cost you gathered earlier. Depending on which site you use you may also need to enter the difficulty and/or network hashrate as well as the mining pool fees.

Examine the results you get. The calculator should tell you how much (if any) profit you can expect under the current network conditions with the hardware you selected. If you like what you see...

Think about the future. Just because the calculator says you can make a profit today doesn't guarantee you'll be in the black next year. Or next week. The mining difficulty changes constantly... almost always by increasing. VnBitcoin (www.vnbitcoin.org/bitcoincalculator.php) not only has yet another mining calculator you can use, but it has information on predicted difficulty rates. Play with the numbers and see how long you'll be profitable with the current rate of increase.

If you've done all of this you've accomplished something that most Bitcoin newcomers never even attempt. Most just assume they can mine profitably and are frustrated when reality (and math) teaches them otherwise. You, however, have run the numbers yourself and proven that you can turn a profit. Now it's up to you to actually make it happen. Start shopping around for deals on the hardware you selected and start learning those mining concepts you ignored earlier.

Setting up a Bitcoin miner after you purchase one is beyond the scope of a beginner's guide. Mining isn't for beginners. It isn't difficult, but it certainly isn't simple. It will require patience and a moderate tolerance for frustration. Between the vendor documentation and the various Bitcoin forums you can find plenty of guidance on getting started. The mining forum on Reddit (www.reddit.com/r/BitcoinMining/) is a good place to go if you run into trouble. Happy Mining.

Mining Alternatives

When confronted with the terrible truth that they can't mine bitcoin with their computers, some Bitcoin newcomers start looking for alternatives. They two they most frequently come across are cloud mining and altcoin mining.

Cloud Mining is just like regular Bitcoin mining, except that instead of buying and running the hardware yourself, you're renting it and paying someone else to run it. Companies like Genesis Mining (www.genesis-mining.com) will sell you a mining contract for certain amount of hashrate. The machines remain in their data centers; you keep the profit. I typically warn people away from cloud mining for two reasons. First is that there have been a number of mining scams that have given the cloud mining industry a black eye. It is far too easy to be taken advantage of. Second is the unwillingness of most people to perform the profitability calculations I detailed earlier in this chapter. That process still applies to cloud mining. But instead of crunching the numbers for themselves, too many people take the marketing hype of cloud mining companies at face value. The result is a disappointing return on investment, or a profit that is driven more by the increase in the bitcoin conversion rate rather than the mining process itself. However, if you do the research and calculations, cloud mining could be a viable alternative to buying hardware yourself. But there are no guarantees.

Bitcoin mining may not be profitable with desktop hardware, but Bitcoin isn't the only cryptocurrency around. There are numerous other currencies that can be mined with standard CPUs and GPUs (graphics cards). Of course, the result of this mining effort wouldn't be bitcoin... it would whatever altcoin you were set up to mine. If it was bitcoin you were after, you'd have to use an exchange or service like Shapeshift to make the conversation. You'll also need to take the exchange's fees into account when you do your profitability calculations.

There is a new altcoin mining pool called Nicehash (new.nicehash.com) that makes the process easy by automatically switching your machine to the most profitable of the altcoins it supports. It also coverts your earnings to bitcoin automatically. With a decent GPU you can easily make a few dollars a day with zero effort beyond the initial setup. With great graphics cards and multiple computers, you can make significantly more. Nicehash even calculates and displays your dollars-per-day in the interface to take some of the effort out of profitability calculations. I am in no way affiliated with Nicehash other than being a user, but based on my experience I recommend it for people who have modern gaming computers that sit idle most of the day.

Chapter Four: Spending Bitcoin

Online Merchants

While the number of establishments that accept bitcoin is still limited compared to traditional currencies, it is growing daily. There are far too many Bitcoin-enabled online merchants to list in this book, but some names among the crowd may surprise you. Major online stores that accept bitcoin include Expedia, Shopify, Microsoft, Dell, Overstock, and the popular gaming platform Steam.

Gift Cards

These merchants, also referred to as 3rd party merchants, sell gift cards that you can buy using bitcoin and use to purchase goods online or offline. Think of them as a bridge that connects bitcoin users with merchants that don't accept bitcoin for payments. The most popular vendor for gift cards is Gyft (www.gyft.com) The number and names of the vendors they support is too long to list, but it contains such names as Amazon.com, Home Depot, Starbucks, Macy's, Best Buy, Lowes, and Target.

Physical Stores

Just because Bitcoin is a product of the digital age doesn't mean you can't use it to shop offline. More and more "brick and mortar" stores all over the world are now accepting bitcoin payments. From building materials to clothes, from coffee and vape shops to restaurants, physical stores are a new frontier for bitcoin acceptance. You can use resources such as Coinmap (coinmap.org) to find offline or physical stores in your area that accept bitcoin wherever you are in the world.

Amazon via Purse.io

Purse.io (www.purse.io) offers a useful and unique service that allows you use bitcoin for items from Amazon.com without having to buy a gift card first. Purse operates similarly to LocalBitcoins, in that it connects people who want to buy something on Amazon (Shoppers) with people who want to turn their currency into bitcoin (Earners). Shoppers create a public wishlist on Amazon and populate it with the item or items they want to purchase. They share the wishlist on Purse.io's website, and deposit enough BTC to cover the purchase. An Earner will purchase the items on the wishlist and have them shipped directly to the shopper. Once the items are received the Earner is reimbursed via the bitcoin deposited by the Shopper. It sounds much more complicated than it is. The fact that, as a Shopper, you have the ability to obtain items at a substantial discount makes it worth trying at least once.

OpenBazaar

OpenBazaar (www.openbazaar.org) is an internet-based peer-to-peer marketplace where anyone can sell any item for bitcoin. OpenBazaar has been compared to both Ebay and the Silk Road, but it is neither of these things. There are no auctions, only peer-to-peer sales. There is nothing secret, dark, or hidden about it or its listings. Unlike both Ebay and the Silk Road, OpenBazaar does not operate on one server or set of servers that can be located and shut down. The marketplace is decentralized, free to use, free from external interference, and a good place to both earn and spend bitcoin.

The Bitcoin Payment Process

Regardless of whether you are buying something online or through a face-to-face transaction, using Bitcoin is easier than using a credit card in most cases.

The person or website receiving the payment will show you a QR Code like the one below pictured below:

The code may look like random squares, but your Bitcoin wallet can pull the payment address and, usually, the payment amount out of the code. All you'll need to do is open your wallet, click "send" or "scan" and point your camera at the code. If the payment amount wasn't included in the code, you'll need to type that in. If you're buying something online, you might not even need to use the camera at all The QR code (or the page that is displaying it) will often have a link that should open your Bitcoin wallet directly and populate the required fields.

Before you hit the final "send or "pay" button, make sure you are including an appropriate fee.

Wait... fees? Yes. Remember those miners that are processing your transactions with their expensive specialized hardware? One of the ways they get paid is the "optional" fee that you include in your transaction. I put optional in quotes because, while it is technically possible to send a Bitcoin transaction with zero fee, few (if any) wallets will allow you to do so. Worse still, a zero- or low-fee transaction may take weeks to be written to the blockchain, if it is ever written at all.

Most wallets will suggest a fee amount that you should include, and some will give you options for a higher or lower fee, depending on how fast you want the transaction to process. This fee is based on the complexity of the transaction, not the amount of dollars or BTC you're sending. It also changes according to the load on the network. During Bitcoin's history the recommended fee has ranged from a tiny fraction of a cent to over $2. As of this writing, the wallet that I use recommends a fee of $1, but has options ranging from $.62 for a "low priority" transactions to $1.25 for a "high-priority" transaction. Keep in mind that the fee is paid in bitcoin, and the dollar amount of that fee will vary with the exchange rate. Just use one of your wallet's suggestions and you'll be fine.

What happens now depends on what fee you paid, what you bought, and how the merchant chooses to do business. A Bitcoin transaction is not considered "confirmed" until it is written to the blockchain. This may take ten minutes, an hour, or ten days, depending on the fee... but 10 minutes should be the average for a transaction with an appropriate fee.

Is the cashier at the coffee shop going to make you wait ten minutes before they hand over your beverage? Of course not. The cashier's wallet will display the incoming (but unconfirmed) transaction almost instantly after you make the payment. If they're savvy, they'll check to make sure you include a fee, but most likely they'll just hand over your beverage and move on to the next person in line.

On the other hand... what if you just bought a $200 gift card, a $2000 computer, or a $10,000 used car? Is the merchant going to allow you to walk (or drive) away with the merchandise without waiting for a confirmation? Of course not. You can expect to sit and discuss sports or the weather while the transaction confirms. This is one of those times you might opt to include a higher-than-normal fee with your transaction.

Chapter Five: Keeping Bitcoin

Bitcoin Wallets

As with traditional currencies, safekeeping of your bitcoin is of paramount importance. But unlike traditional currencies the job of securing your wealth is entirely on your shoulders. The fact that bitcoin is entirely digital makes securing them even more difficult. People inherently know how to keep physical objects safe. Securing digital files, however, is outside of most people's area of expertise... until they get hacked. With potentially life-changing amounts of money at stake, learning basic Bitcoin security by trial and error is not acceptable. It is imperative you learn how to store your bitcoin before you start buying or investing large amounts.

Bitcoins are stored in addresses. Multiple addresses are collected in and controlled by wallets. Wallets are usually (but not always) software programs running on a phone or computer. With proper safety practices and mechanisms, these wallets can be safer than your physical wallet, bank account, and credit cards. Without these basic security measures, however, bitcoin wallets are like keeping a bag of money half-hidden behind a flowerpot on your front porch.

There are four kinds of Bitcoin wallets that you can choose from: web wallets, software wallets, cold storage wallets, and hardware wallets.

Software or "hot" wallets are the ones you will interact with most often. This is the Bitcoin wallet on your phone or computer that you use for buying, selling, and transferring BTC. There are several companies producing wallets for the various platforms. I recommend Mycelium on Android and Breadwallet on iOS. For PC, I recommend Electrum. My two rules for choosing a wallet are: 1) Do not pay for wallet software. It should be free. 2) Do not store large amounts of money in a hot wallet. Software wallets are the equivalent of petty cash or the money you carry around in your pocket. They are not a savings account, so don't put thousands of dollars into one unless you are about to make a large purchase in the very near future.

A web wallet is a software wallet hosted on an online server and usually accessed through a web browser. There are some very popular and trustworthy companies that will store your bitcoin for you in their online servers. I'm not naming them because you should avoid all of them. That's right... all of them. The short history of Bitcoin is filled with online wallets that got careless or turned out to be scams, resulting in the unreimbursed loss of their clients' funds. Learn from other people's mistakes: *Do Not Store Bitcoin In An Online Wallet.* This includes the wallets run by the exchanges where you buy bitcoin. You can trust them to buy or sell your bitcoin, but you should not trust them to store it for you.

Cold Storage wallets, also referred to as offline wallets, are wallets that are totally removed from a hosting device or the Internet. This can be an old computer or phone that you've loaded some Bitcoin software onto and disconnected from the internet. The average user will typically only put this machine online long enough to transfer funds from the cold wallet into their hot wallet... similar to taking money out of a savings account into a checking account. This is where the bulk of your bitcoin should be kept. Note that the platform... the phone or PC that you are using... must be secure and must only be used for Bitcoin. Wiping the operating system and starting with a fresh, virus-free re-install is recommended. Using the device to browse the web, read books, watch porn, update your resume, or anything else will get your bitcoin stolen out from under you.

Hardware wallets are a special type of cold storage. These are specific hardware devices... physical objects... that you can use to store bitcoin and access it securely even from a computer that isn't itself secure. If you are dealing with life-changing amounts of money, then you should invest in one of these. Otherwise, ordinary cold storage wallets on an old phone or PC may suffice.

Paper wallets are yet another special type of cold storage. As the name suggests, a paper wallet stores your bitcoin address and private key on an ordinary piece of paper. You use a computer and a printer to create the paper wallet and a normal hot wallet to send bitcoin to/from the address encoded on the page. While the bitcoin is at rest it is completely isolated from the internet and invulnerable to attack... unless you loose the paper wallet or didn't follow instructions when you created it. Paper wallets are very useful, and were the only hardware wallets available until companies like Ledger and Trezor came along. But they are not user friendly. They are too easy to use incorrectly, and using them the right way can be awkward. Nevertheless, they are worth exploring if you will be storing large amounts of BTC and don't want to purchase special hardware to do so. They can at the very least be a temporary storage measure while your hardware wallet is being shipped. If you want to play around with paper wallets visit BitAddress (www.bitaddress.org). Warning: Going to a website and printing off a paper wallet is insecure. It's fine for learning and experimenting, but not for actual use. Creating a **secure** paper wallet involves multiple steps and a moderate amount of paranoia. Also, never buy paper wallets from anyone. Always create your own.

Preparing for Bitcoin

Cold storage or hardware wallets either cost money or require you to have an extra machine sitting around that you can dedicate to Bitcoin. Paper wallets are free, but they are confusing and take time to create correctly. These may not be suitable options for everyone, so some may choose to store their bitcoin on their ordinary phone or computer. While this this isn't recommended, it is understandable and almost certainly the route that most new users will take. Given the higher risks associated with software wallets, you will need to exercise extra caution when using them for storing larger amounts.

Entire libraries have been written on how to secure computers. The unfortunate truth is that the average user will never read even one of those books and, if they did, probably wouldn't follow the recommendations it contains. For that reason, I'm going to scale down all of that very good advice to the absolute bare minimum you need to do. If you perform any financial transactions on your phone or PC... either with bitcoin or your regular banking/investing website... you should do the following:

Put a passcode or password on your machine. It doesn't need to be long, but it does need to be complex. Uppercase, lowercase, special characters... the more complex the better. Hopefully, you are already doing this.

Use some kind of anti-virus or anti-malware. If you have Windows, use the Windows Defender that comes with the operating system. There are several for Android; consider Malwarebytes or Lookout. The latter comes already installed on a lot of newer Android devices. Whatever you use, it should not only scan the device periodically for malware on the hard drive, it should also actively monitor activity on the device in an attempt to catch malware in the act.

I find Apple's operating systems for its devices like the MacBook, iPad, and the iPhone to be quite virus and malware-resistant. However, Apple's electronic products are significantly more expensive than Windows-based computer devices, Android phones, and Android tablets.

The last bit of advice is for Windows users only. It is also crucial for that platform. If you are like most people you only have one account on your machine, and that account is an administrator. This means that the account you use while surfing the internet is also able to manage the settings, install software, and make changes to the machine's configuration... exactly the things that a virus or trojan wants to do once it hits your machine. You need to fix that. The account that you use every day should not be an administrator. You need to create a second account that you only log into when you are installing or configuring something. This new account should be the administrator while your everyday computer use should just be done under a "standard" account.

These simple steps, particularly the last one, will go a long way toward making your computer safe enough for financial use.

Choosing and Setting Up a Wallet

Now it's time to choose your Bitcoin software wallet. If you want to do your own research instead of just picking one of the ones I mentioned earlier, go to bitcoin.org/en/choose-your-wallet and click around. All Bitcoin software wallets are not created equal. Even if all the features and security were the same among them, there are still vast differences in initial setup and ease of use. Bitcoin Core, for example, requires you to download the entire Bitcoin blockchain before you can use it. That might sound okay until you realize that the blockchain is over 120GB and will take over a week to download. New users don't need that level of frustration, so I recommend you avoid Bitcoin Core.

After successfully setting up the software wallet in your chosen electronic device, you'll need to work on the software settings before using it. The two most important settings that you should pay attention to are your wallet's password and backup system.

If the software lets you create a PIN or password to access your wallet, you should set one. This should be different from the one you use to unlock your PC, phone or tablet. Your software may also present you with a list of random words that allow you to restore your wallet when needed. Write the words down... physically, on paper... and store them somewhere safe. These random words are literally the keys to your Bitcoin kingdom. Do not store them on (or near) your computer; they belong in a safe, safe deposit box, or other secure storage place that is both fire and waterproof.

Address Management

Once you've set up your first Bitcoin wallet, look for your Bitcoin addresses. All software is different, but since address management is the entire point of the wallet, the software should display them prominently. You have more than one address. If you only see one, rest assured that your wallet can create additional addresses with the click of a button.

When receiving bitcoin, such as when you are transferring newly purchased BTC out of an exchange, you will need to provide one of your address. Please don't try to memorize or type an address by hand, use copy/paste.

You should generate a new address every time you need to receiver bitcoin. *Do Not Re-Use Addresses*. Once you use an address to receive BTC once... forget about it. Don't worry, it's the wallet software's job to keep track of how much BTC is in each address, not yours. Using different addresses makes it more difficult for people to track your Bitcoin activity on the blockchain.

Hardware Wallets

As mentioned earlier, hardware wallets are the most secure way to store your bitcoin. While there aren't as many hardware wallets as software wallets, there are still too many to list and describe in detail. Instead, I'll focus on the two most popular ones.

 Trezor (trezor.io) is a dongle that plugs into the USB port of your computer. You access it via your web browser using special software or a browser extension that you obtain from Trezor. The interface is much like a regular software wallet, but behind the scenes it is using a lot of encryption to isolate your wallet (and the bitcoin it contains) from the computer you plug it into. The Trezor retails at $100 on the Trezor website, but supplies are limited and the prices at 3rd party vendors are $175 to $200 USD. When you shop for one, be prepared to find many vendors with limited stock and higher prices.

Ledger (www.ledgerwallet.com) sells the Ledger Nano S as a hardware wallet that operates similarly to the Trezor. It can integrate with existing wallet software such as Mycelium, and be used with a small list altcoins besides Bitcoin, such as Litecoin and Ethereum. It is also slightly cheaper, retailing at $70 on Ledger's website.

For use with Bitcoin, the differences between these two are largely cosmetic. Choose whichever you can afford or whichever you can actually find in stock. If you are doing research online, be aware that Ledger produced a previous version of their hardware wallet that lacked many features. Reviewers generally considered inferior to the Trezor, but those reviews don't apply to the current Ledger Nano S.

When you first get your hardware wallet, do your best to ascertain that it is brand new, i.e., it hasn't been used or tampered in any way prior to your receiving it. There have been instances when customs agents and authorities have opened shipments and in the process, removed security seals of the items contained in such shipments. Remember, your bitcoins' security will depend on the integrity of your hardware wallet and as such, it must arrive on your doorstep in a pristine and unmodified state.

Once you're satisfied that your hardware wallet is genuine and hadn't been tampered with, you'll go through the initial setup that is similar to setting up a software wallet. There are passwords to set and lists of random words to write down. Do so and enjoy using Bitcoin is the most secure way possible.

Chapter Six: Investing in Bitcoin

Disclaimer: *I am not a financial or investment adviser. This chapter is general advice only. It has been prepared without taking into account your objectives, financial situation or needs. Before acting on this advice you should consider its appropriateness in regard to your own objectives, financial situation and needs. Regardless of what I or anyone else says, you should never invest in something you do not understand, or invest funds you cannot afford to lose.*

While Bitcoin was created as an alternative and decentralized mode of payment, it can also be used as an investment. Bitcoin had zero value when it was initially released in January of 2009. Shortly thereafter it had a value of .08 cents per bitcoin, mostly based on the amount of electricity required to mine BTC at the time. In mid-2017 the value of 1 Bitcoin peaked at $3,000.

Upon hearing the previous figures, most people have one of two reactions. Some feel that they have obviously "missed the boat" on Bitcoin and that there's no point in investing now. Others see the exponential rise as an obvious sign that Bitcoin is a scam. Neither of these is true,, but it can be difficult to change minds without delving into Bitcoin's history and the true meaning of its technology.

But first, let's attack some of the more popular objections to Bitcoin investing.

One of the reasons why many people fear investing in, or even using, Bitcoin is the infamous bankruptcy of one of the biggest Bitcoin exchanges in the world, Mt. Gox in 2014, which preceded a precipitous drop in price. Many proclaimed Bitcoin to be "dead" at this point. Yet, Bitcoin still exists and is trading a significantly higher price than it was in 2014. In fact, Bitcoin has "died" so often that it has become a meme or joke in the Bitcoin community. The collapse of Mt Gox is a historical footnote among a sea of other hacks and collapses... none of which have "killed" cryptocurrency. These were not failures of Bitcoin or of cryptocurrency any more than the Cyprus financial crisis of 2012 was a failure of fiat currency.

Another black mark is Bitcoin's association with scams, frauds, and black market activities such as the Bitcoin Savings and Trust Ponzi scheme and the Silk Road dark market. Yet the same people who decry Bitcoin's reputation continue to use a currency with a much longer history of even stronger ties to illegal activity: Cash... the currency of drug dealers, pedophiles, and black markets since before the internet existed. Despite rumors to the contrary, Bitcoin is NOT anonymous and people who use Bitcoin for illegal activities do get caught and convicted. The investigation of their activities just takes a different set of skills. Criminals who are serious about keeping their transactions under the radar will do as they always have... use cash.

Another reason for the skepticism is the high volatility in the market value or prices of Bitcoin, which is about 2,600% more volatile than investing in the S&P 500, one of the biggest stock exchanges in the United States and in the world. Yes, Bitcoin is volatile. But that volatility isn't just random noise... it has a very sharp upward trend with discernible patterns. This is what true investors call an opportunity.

And finally, Bitcoin's lack of regulatory body or agency scares people. It's hard for an outsider to see who controls Bitcoin. Is it the government? The Federal Reserve? The Bitcoin Foundation? The mysterious Satoshi Nakamoto? No. Bitcoin (the technology) is controlled by the actions of the developers, miners and users... the Bitcoin community. The bitcoin price is controlled by the free market forces of supply and demand. Let's not forget that the maximum supply of Bitcoin is known and capped at $21 million. The maximum number of US Dollars is infinite. This makes Bitcoin fundamentally different from all traditional currencies. It is more akin to gold and silver, with advantages of being more resistant to government and corporate interference and being able to be used over the internet.

Given the above, should you use Bitcoin for investing purposes? Unfortunately, the answer is neither clear nor simple. The short version of the answer is: "It Depends". The long answer is that, you'll need to consider several things about your own goals, financial situation, and personality before making a decision.

Financial Timeline

While it's obvious that the goal of investing is to make more money, that is a very general goal and is insufficient for actually making investment decisions.

You need to be specific in your expected return, and even more so in your time frame. Are you investing money so you can have a retirement fund in twenty years? Is it for your kids' college education in ten years? Or is it for the new car you're going to buy in a few months?

Bitcoin is NOT a suitable short term investment. If you need to jump in and out of your investment in time frames shorter than a year, you'd be better off looking elsewhere. Bitcoin's strength is its long-term trend. In the short term, the volatility could bite you. Hard. I consider short-term Bitcoin investing to be the same as gambling. Yes, people make money day trading or short-term investing in bitcoin. People also win at blackjack.

If, however, your investment timeline is measured in years, then Bitcoin might be for you.

Risk Appetite

Bitcoin is a high-risk investment. Don't let anyone tell you otherwise.

How much money are you comfortable losing? No one intends to lose money, but all investments have risks. The only question is how much risk can you take. If you want to earn substantially higher returns, you must be willing to accept more risk. Experienced investors know this, but Bitcoin has a tendency to attract inexperienced or amateur investors who expect high returns without the potential for loss. Don't be an amateur. If you ARE an amateur... Bitcoin probably isn't for you. Bitcoin should not be the first or only investment in your portfolio.

If you prefer investments whose returns are guaranteed, consider Treasury Bonds issued by the Federal Government. However, you must be willing to settle for rates of return so low that you may actually lose money because of inflation. But if you are willing to take on higher investment risks to earn potentially higher returns, then you can invest your money in riskier assets like stocks and bitcoin.

Emotional Stability

Suppose you bought some bitcoin today at $2500, and tomorrow the price drops to $1400. It may not be likely, but stranger things have certainly happened. Whether you sell or hold depends on your investment strategy, but that's not the question I'm asking. What about you? Can you handle the emotional reaction to such a stunning potential loss? How would you handle it? Would you panic? Would you take it in stride and move on? Would you obsess over the price, checking it constantly in search of validation? Would you ask, then beg, then plead with strangers on the internet to magically predict when the price will go back up? Would you sink into depression? Would you consider harming yourself?

This may be an unexpectedly dark section to find in a chapter on investment, but some people are emotionally unprepared for the stunning losses that have occurred in Bitcoin's past. As I said earlier, Bitcoin tends to attract people who are new to investing These people tend to invest too much and are not capable of maintaining perspective if things don't go their way. Don't be one of them. There are more important things in the world than money... Bitcoin or otherwise. If your happiness, your survival, your financial or emotional stability depend on the price of an investment behaving in a certain manner... please stay away from Bitcoin.

Timing

Lastly, one universal aspect of trading in financial assets like stocks, currencies, and of course bitcoin, is knowing when to get in and when to get out. There are two approaches to investing that you can take: a buy-and-hold approach and a trading approach.

A buy-and-hold approach is one where you buy bitcoin and wait for its value to go up over the medium to long term. It's also called a buy-it-and-forget-it approach because you don't need to concern yourself with daily or even weekly fluctuations. This approach requires a long-term mindset and, in the specific case of bitcoin, nerves of steel as you wait out short term drops in value. With Bitcoin, those short-term drops can be quite dramatic.

The trading approach is a very short-term one, where you get in and out of bitcoin in a few days, hours, or even minutes. Some people make a killing out of this approach but this requires a lot of time and effort to monitor and execute. It is not for amateurs, and I don't even recommend it for professional traders unless they've educated themselves on the history and technology of Bitcoin.

But even if you take the buy-and-hold approach, it doesn't mean you're off the hook in terms of timing your entry into the market. Should you invest everything at once, or invest over time? Should you buy right now at whatever the price happens to be, or wait until one of those short-term drops?

The answer depends on how much risk you can swallow, financially and emotionally.

If you have a lump sum and won't be shaken by an unexpected drop, invest all at once. You are missing out on potential gains if you wait. If you don't have a lump sum, or the idea of a $400 price drop after you hit "buy" scares you, then invest a specific dollar amount every week or month until you reach your investment goal... but start right now.

Holding your dollars waiting for a short-term drop is generally a bad idea. You don't know how long you'll be waiting, or whether the price dip you are expecting will happen at all. Either buy now, or buy over time beginning right now. I also don't recommend borrowing money to invest in BTC. Don't mortgage your house. Don't take out a bank loan or borrow against your retirement plan. You either have the money to invest or you don't. If you don't, then buying over time is your best option.

In short: *The best time to buy bitcoin was 2009. The second best time to buy bitcoin is right now.*

And finally, once you've acquired Bitcoins for the purpose of investing, be sure to follow the safety protocols for storing your bitcoin that I've outlined earlier in the book. For long-term storage of large amounts, use a cold wallet, hardware wallet, or paper wallet. Storing your investment on a phone wallet is **extremely** unwise.

Author's Notes: What's Next?

Thank you for buying this book. My goal in writing it was to provide enough basic guidance to get you started with Bitcoin... or at least enough to get you interested. I urge you now to take action on what you've learned. Regardless of whether you are a potential investor, merchant, miner, developer or educator, your next steps are the same. Ready? Here they are:

Buy some bitcoin. Spend some of it. Save the rest.

That's it. Doing this with just a small amount of bitcoin, $10 to $100 dollars worth, will start cementing and internalizing what you've learned in this book. You'll work with an exchange. You'll find and install a wallet. You'll locate a merchant that accepts bitcoin in exchange for something you want. You'll experience the importance of fees. And you'll have a tiny bit of bitcoin stashed away in case of another 10- or 100-fold increase in value. All of this was described in this book, but no amount of explanation is as good as firsthand experience. So go ahead... use Bitcoin the way it was meant to be used. From there you can branch out into your specific areas of interest, be it mining or investing, starting a bitcoin-based business or charity, or using Bitcoin to send money overseas.

Even if you decide Bitcoin isn't for you, you'll have made that decision based on personal experience rather than a preconceived notion. Don't worry, cryptocurrencies like Bitcoin aren't going anywhere. They'll still be here when you change your mind. And you **will** change your mind.

Until then,

Thanks for Reading

Eric Morse

Bitcoin:
A Concise History

A Timeline of Bitcoin's Defining Moments

By

Eric Morse

"You can't know where you are going until you know where you have been"
--unknown

"Those who cannot remember the past are condemned to repeat it."
--George Santayana

Table of Contents

Introduction

Why A Bitcoin Timeline?

Bitcoin is many things. It is a currency (or "cash for the internet"). It is a decentralized network protocol that makes the currency work ("the internet of money"). And it is a community of users, developers, investors both professional and amateur. There are many of books about the technology of Bitcoin and its associated technologies. There are almost none about its history or how the current community and ecosystem evolved from it. As the quotes at the beginning of this book imply, I feel that knowing where you came from is necessary to understand where you're going... and why.

The following pages present a timeline of Bitcoin, from before the early days of Satoshi Nakamoto's white paper, through scams and scandals of MtGox and Bitcoin Savings and Trust, through the rise and fall (and rise and fall...) of the bitcoin price and the birth of popular memes that confound new users to this day.

At the end, you may understand Bitcoin (the currency) a little better. But you will understand Bitcoin (the community) a LOT better.

But why?

Why would I write such a book? Who is the target audience? Who will get the most out of it?

Potential Investors. Understanding the events that shaped Bitcoin's current state is of paramount importance to anyone who is (or will be) putting money into Bitcoin, either by investing directly in the currency or by starting Bitcoin-related businesses. Investors need to know WHY things are the way they are so that they can spot trouble, hopefully before it happens. This timeline will spell out events that either caused or correlated with significant price movement. Since Bitcoin is so new, there isn't much history from which patterns and conclusions can be drawn... investors need to study every bit of it, lest they be doomed to repeat some of the more unpleasant bits.

End Users. While not quite as crucial as for investors, end users (including merchants) also need an understanding of Bitcoin's history... but for a different reason. Bitcoin derives much (some say all) of its value from the community. End users become a part of that community in a way that is not true of people who spend dollars, euros, or Visa Gift cards. If for no other reason, end users need some concept Bitcoin's history so that they understand the WHY behind the instructions and advice they receive when they turn to the community for help. They will be told, for instance, that they should never leave bitcoin in an online wallet. This timeline gives several stunning examples why.

Educators, Legislators, and Spectators. Much like end users, people who view the Bitcoin community from the outside need a background in order to understand why the community acts and reacts the way it does. Anyone who seeks to change Bitcoin (the community OR the currency) should know what happened to those who tried it before. There is a solid core of the community that is anti-authoritarian and distrustful of politicians, even (or especially) those with good intentions. You will find out why. You will also see some entertaining examples of folly, karma, tragedy, and drunken internet postings that became immortalized in the collective memory of Bitcoin.

So, who should read this book? Everyone. Either for entertainment or necessity, anyone with the slightest interest in Bitcoin has something to discover in this timeline. I've tried to make it as useful as I can for all of you. The prerequisites are simple: Curiosity, and general, non-technical idea of what Bitcoin is. The timeline contains some techno-speak out of necessity, but I try to explain everything as I move long. If you are brand new to Bitcoin... you literally just heard about it last week, for instance... I recommend starting with my previous book: Bitcoin, A simple Introduction to get up to speed.

Ready for the ride? Let's Go!

Eric Morse.

Chapter 1: Precursors, Predecessors, and Predictions

Bitcoin was not created in a vacuum, nor was it the first attempt at a digital currency for the internet. To understand Bitcoin, one must understand the world in which it was created and the problems that Bitcoin was intended to solve.

August 15, 1971
As part of his New Economic Policy program, US President Richard Nixon ends the convertibility of US dollars (USD) to gold. This act converts the dollar (and other currencies that had been pegged to it since 1944) into fiat currencies. Since from 1971 to 2017, the cumulative rate of inflation of the US dollar has been over 500%. An item that cost $100 USD in 1971 would cost over $600 in 2017.

March 9, 1993

Eric Hughes publishes The Cypherpunk's Manifesto, a statement of intent and philosophy from a group of coders and technophiles known as the Cypherpunks. The manifesto venerates privacy and stresses the need for systems allowing users to communicate and transact while remaining anonymous. The development of "electronic money" is specifically named as a key goal. While there is no direct connection between this group and Bitcoin, the manifesto can be considered a spiritual predecessor to Satoshi Nakamoto's white paper. The original Cypherpunk Manifesto is archived here: **https://w2.eff.org/Privacy/Crypto/Crypto_misc/cypherpun k.manifesto**

Late 1996
Douglas Jackson and Barry Downey found E-Gold, a company that provides the instantaneous transfer of gold ownership over the internet. The gold itself remained in vaults owned and secured by E-Gold. E-Gold is considered the world's first successful digital currency. E-Gold's operators will claim their system served millions of users in dozens of countries before the government shuts them down in 2009 for money laundering and operating as an unlicensed money transmitter. Bitcoin's early detractors would point to E-Gold's fate as an example of what would eventually befall Bitcoin. **Spoiler Alert: They were wrong.**

July 2, 2001
Developer and cypherpunk Bram Cohen releases the first BitTorrent client. BitTorrent is a peer-to-peer file sharing protocol that, while bearing no relation to Bitcoin, is important in that its decentralized nature has made it resistant to government and corporate attempts to regulate its use. Bitcoin is to money transmission what BitTorrent is to file sharing.

August 18, 2008

The domain "www.bitcoin.org" is anonymously registered through anonymousspeech.com, a website that does not reveal the identity of its clients.

October 31, 2008
Satoshi Nakamoto (a pseudonym) publishes Bitcoin: A Peer-to-Peer Electronic Cash System, a white paper describing a peer-to-peer monetary system that could operate over the internet without the interference or permission of 3rd parties. It is a form of decentralized electronic cash... Cash for the Internet. The word "Bitcoin" refers to both the network ("Bitcoin") and the currency upon which it operates ("bitcoin" or "BTC"). Bitcoin transactions are written in blocks that are appended to a public decentralized ledger (the blockchain) that tracks bitcoin ownership. Unlike E-Gold and similar to BitTorrent, there is no Bitcoin "company" to shut down or "CEO" to arrest... there is only the network. Unlike fiat currencies, the amount of bitcoin is capped at 21 million, making it inflation-proof. Satoshi Nakamoto's original Bitcoin wite paper can be found at: **https://bitcoin.org/bitcoin.pdf**

Chapter 2: 2009- Year One

Price of BTC on January 1, 2010: N/A
The launch of Bitcoin in January 2009 introduced a
revolutionary technology that was largely ignored by the public.
Behind the scenes, however, a small segment of the technophile
community takes notice.

January 3, 2009
 Satoshi Nakamoto mines the first block in the Bitcoin
blockchain, also known as the genesis block.

January 9, 2009
Six days following the mining of the genesis block, creator
Satoshi Nakamoto releases the Bitcoin source code and his
Bitcoin client. The client, Bitcoin 0.1, is downloaded by
programmer Hal Finney, who uses it to receive the first Bitcoin
transaction of 10 BTC. Bitcoin has no monetary value at this
point, but today those 10 BTC would be worth over $25,000.

October 5, 2009

New Liberty Standard (a technology website) publishes an exchange rate for Bitcoin to dollars -- 1.309.03 BTC per dollar, or about .08 cents each. The rate is based on the computing power and electricity required to generate bitcoin.

October 12, 2009
New Liberty Standard uses PayPal to buy 5,050 BTC for the price of $5.02. This places the exchange rate of .1 cents each per bitcoin.
Also on this day, #bitcoin-dev becomes available on Internet Relay Chat (IRC). It will eventually be joined and then overshadowed by the BitcoinTalk forum and multiple forums on Reddit.com.

November 22, 2009
Satoshi Nakamoto establishes The BitcoinTalk Forum on a subdirectory of bitcoin.org. The forum will move to its own domain, bitcointalk.org, in 2011. BitcoinTalk will serve as a vital source of news, discussion, debate, and important announcements for the Bitcoin community, and will remain relevant even after alternative news sources come into being.

December 16, 2009
Bitcoin 0.2 is released. It is compatible with both Windows and Linux.

December 30, 2009
The first Bitcoin mining difficulty increase occurs. Mining is the process of writing blocks of transactions to the blockchain using, in the beginning, standard computer CPUs. Miners compete with one another to perform complex encryption calculations, and the first to do so writes the block and earns a 50 bitcoin mining reward. The amount of this reward (in BTC) decreases over time. Bitcoin attempts to maintain a 1 block per 10 minute mining rate by increasing the difficulty of the calculations as the number of miners increase. There will be many such increases; this one is

significant because it is the first, and because it indicates growing interest in mining bitcoin.

Chapter 3: 2010- A Bigger Pond

Price of BTC on January 1, 2010: $0.01
While Bitcoin's appeal is still largely confined to a small community, it is beginning to receive recognition by other groups, leading to its first tenfold rise in value.

February 6, 2010
A Bitcoin user nicknamed 'dwdollar' establishes Bitcoin Market, an online exchange. The website displays a real-time exchange rate between Bitcoin and the dollar. Users could make purchases using PayPal until 2011.

May 22, 2010
On the BitcoinTalk Forum, Laszlo Hanyecz offers 10,000 BTC to someone who would order him a pizza. User 'jercos' takes him up on the offer and orders him two pizzas from Papa John's for $25. The exchange rate for this transaction is .25 cents per bitcoin. Today, 10,000 BTC would be worth millions of dollars. May 22 is known humorously as "Bitcoin Pizza Day" in honor of this transaction.

July 7, 2010
Bitcoin version 0.3 is released.

July 11, 2010
Bitcoin is mentioned on www.slashdot.com, a technology news website. The short article notes that the value of a bitcoin is already higher than the energy required to produce it, leading to a massive increase in interest in the currency. Within five days, the value of a bitcoin increased tenfold from .8 cents to 8 cents.

July 17, 2010
Jed McCaleb establishes the Bitcoin exchange Mt. Gox, which would become the largest Bitcoin exchange in the world. The name refers to "Magic: The Gathering Online Exchange," as McCaleb initially created the site as an exchange for MtG trading cards.

August 15, 2010
Hackers use a vulnerability in the Bitcoin software to produce 184 billion BTC. Developers patch the vulnerability and address the problem of the billions of extraneous BTC by forking the blockchain at a point prior to when the exploit occurred. In layman's terms, users and developers pick a point in the ledger and start over from there, invalidating all transactions after that point.

September 9, 2010
The subreddit "r/bitcoin" is created on the popular Reddit platform. The main moderator is Michael Marquardt, aka "theymos", who is also a moderator (and current owner) of the BitcoinTalk forum.

October 2010
The Financial Action Task Force issues a report highlighting what it saw as the dangers of online currencies, including Bitcoin. The dangers stem from the anonymity of users, which

could allow individuals to use Bitcoin to fund terrorism without detection. It also mentions the lack of governmental regulation and oversight, and the potential for monetary abuse including tax evasion and money laundering. The Bitcoin community considers many of these dangers to be "features".

October 17, 2010
#bitcoin-otc debuts on IRC for the purpose of buying and selling bitcoin.

November 6, 2010
The total value of all existing bitcoin reaches one million dollars. In the thirteen months since New Liberty Standard set the exchange rate at .08 cents each, bitcoin increased in value over a hundredfold.

December 3, 2010
Paypal, a popular online payment portal, announces that they will stop processing payments for Wikileaks, a non-profit media organization that publishes secret, classified, and leaked information. Visa and Mastercard quickly follow suit, leaving Wikileaks unable to accept donations. This sparks a series of cyber-attacks against Visa, Mastercard and Paypal, as well as discussions of whether Bitcoin can be used to circumvent the financial blockade.

December 12, 2010
On this day, Satoshi Nakamoto makes his last contribution to the BitcoinTalk Forum. Although some have stepped forward claiming to be Satoshi Nakamoto, the true identity of the creator of Bitcoin remains a mystery.

Chapter 4: 2011- The First Bubble

Price of BTC on January 1, 2011: $0.30
Bitcoin continues to rise in both public awareness and price, and
then suddenly loses most of its value. Bitcoin begins to enter pop
culture when it is mentioned in an episode of The Good Wife and
featured in Time Magazine. Bitcoin's pseudo-anonymity and lack
of traditional financial regulation are exploited in illicit,
underground markets. Several websites and services are
launched that would later become key parts of the Bitcoin
ecosystem... and exemplify its amateur "wild-west" nature.

January 27, 2011
Ross Ulbricht launches the website Silk Road, an illicit market for
trading illegal drugs. The site exists on the supposedly
anonymous TOR network (itself a product of the US
Government) and is named after the ancient trade route that
connected China with the rest of the world. Bitcoin is the
preferred method of payment for goods and services.

January 28, 2011

The total number of bitcoin generated by miners reaches 5.25 million, 25% of the 21 million BTC cap.

February 9, 2011
Bitcoin reaches parity with the US Dollar on the MtGox website (1 BTC= 1 USD). This sparks more interest in the currency as well as concerns from national governments. Subsequent days see such an increase in traffic on MtGox that it could barely cope with the surge of visitors.
Popular Cybersecurity podcast Security Now features an episode devoted almost entirely to Bitcoin.

March 2011
During the month of March 2011, the Bitcoin Market website is significantly renovated to keep up with the surge of demand in the online crypto-currency. Users are now able to exchange at all hours of the day or night; facilitating exchange across time zones and further establishing Bitcoin as a global currency. Furthermore, the minimum required to trade in BTC over the website is lowered.

March 6, 2011
Jed McCaleb, the creator of Mt. Gox, sells the website to the Japan-based French developer Mark Karpelès. Karpelès and MtGox will go on to become infamous.

March 27, 2011
On this day, Britcoin, an online exchange market that trades between BTC and the fiat British pound sterling, is established. The exchange rate is initially valued at approximately 0.5 pounds per bitcoin.

March 31, 2011
Bitcoin Brazil is established to facilitate exchange between BTC and Brazilian Reals. The exchange rate is initially valued at approximately 1.3 Reals per bitcoin.

April 5, 2011

BitMarket.eu is established to facilitate exchange between BTC and Eurodollars. The exchange rate is initially valued at approximately 0.5 Eurodollars per bitcoin.

April 16, 2011

Time Magazine publishes "Online Cash Bitcoin Could Challenge Governments, Banks," an article by Jerry Brito. The article mentions the potential for the unregulated, peer-to-peer currency to bypass the financial blockade of Wikileaks enacted late the previous year. It also highlights some of the Bitcoin-associated challenges facing governments, as well as possible regulatory efforts that may soon be implemented. The article generates much public interest in the currency, who's value begins to to skyrocket.

April 23, 2011

The value of Bitcoin against the Eurodollar and the British pound sterling, according to the Mt. Gox exchange, reaches full parity, making one Bitcoin worth one Eurodollar.
The total value of all bitcoin in circulation surpasses $10 million.

June 1, 2011

News website Gawker publishes an article entitled "The Underground Website Where You Can Buy Any Drug Imaginable," which describes how Bitcoin is used to purchase drugs available through the illicit Silk Road website. The article includes a clickable link that takes users to the Mt. Gox website.

June 2, 2011

The value of Bitcoin reaches $10 USD, just two months after it reached parity with the dollar. This tenfold increase occurs just one day after the Gawker article. The BTC value will continue to surge over the next few weeks.

June 4, 2011

The Bitcoin website discontinues the use of PayPal due to rampant fraud in Paypal payments.

June 8, 2011
BTC reaches $31.91; having tripled in less than one week since the release of the Gawker article. The total value of all BTC in circulation now exceeds $200 million.

TradeHill, a new BTC exchange, is launched. It will become the second-largest Bitcoin exchange in the world.

June 12, 2011
The value of Bitcoin plummets to $4 USD. This drop, known as the Great Bubble of 2011, fails to shake confidence in the currency. Demand for BTC climbs, causing it to regain and exceed its previous value in subsequent weeks.

June 13, 2011
BitcoinTalk forum user Allinvain announces the theft of 25,000 BTC from an unencrypted Bitcoin wallet running on his computer. The loss is noteworthy due to the amount stolen, and the actions of the Bitcoin community in an attempt to track the movement of the stolen BTC. The funds are never recovered, however.

June 14, 2011
Wikileaks begins accepting bitcoin donations. Credit card donations will return in 2013, but a Bitcoin address remains prominently displayed on the Wikileaks donation page. To date, Wikileaks has received over 4024 BTC at their main donation address. This does not include donations made to other addresses controlled by Wikileaks.

June 15, 2011
Mt. Gox is hacked, possibly by a someone accessing the account of an auditor. The hacker attempts to sell a large amount of BTC which causes the exchange rate to plummet to one cent, allowing others to purchase BTC at an artificially low price. The hack also

compromises the email addresses, passwords, and other sensitive information associated with user accounts. This information will later be released to the public. The administrators of Mt. Gox reverse the fraudulent transactions before closing down for several days to update security.
In response to the Mt. Gox hack, Britcoin and Tradehill suspend trading activities until tighter security measures could be implemented.

July 28, 2011
On this day, the Bitcoin exchange Kraken is established. Though small under the shadow of the growing Mt. Gox exchange, Kraken would become the largest Eurodollar-based exchange for Bitcoin.

August 2011
Bitstamp, a Luxembourg-based Bitcoin exchange company, is launched by entrepreneurs Nejc Kodrič and Damijan Merlak.

August 23, 2011
Entrepreneurs Charlie Shrem and Gareth Nelson launch BitInstant, a startup that allows for rapid-service Bitcoin purchases. BitInstant enables clients to purchase BTC by depositing funds into accounts at major banks in over-the-counter transactions. However, the company received many complaints that the rapid transactions actually took several days to process.

August 30, 2011
The blockchain.info website launches. The site is contains real-time statistics and market information on Bitcoin as a currency, such as its current value against other currencies and the total value of all BTC in circulation. It also contains information to help new users get started with Bitcoin. It remains the go-to resource for viewing transactions on the blockchain.

Septmeber 8, 2011

Bitcoinica, an online high-risk, high-reward trading platform, is launched by a 17-year-old Singaporean named Zhou Tong.

October 7, 2011
Litecoin debuts. Litecoin is an alternative cryptocurrency (or "altcoin") based on Bitcoin's source code with modifications to yield a faster block generation time (2.5 minutes), greater maximum number of coins (84 million), and a different hashing algorithm. An explosion of altcoins will soon follow.

November 2011
Trendon Shavers, aka "pirateat40" opens Bitcoin Savings and Trust, advertising a weekly interest rate of 7%. This rate would allow investors' funds to double every 10 weeks. Despite being an obvious Ponzi scheme, there are no shortage of depositors.

December 19, 2011
American TV show The Good Wife announces an episode called "Bitcoin for Dummies," loosely based on the cryptocurrency. In this episode, a lawyer takes on and defends the founder of Bitcoin. The lawyer is arrested for refusing to divulge the name of the client wanted by the Department of the Treasury for creating a new currency competing with the dollar. Though fictional, this episode led to even more exposure and interest in Bitcoin. There does not appear to have been a corresponding increase in price.

Chapter 5: 2012- Essential Groundwork

Price of BTC on January 1, 2012: $5.27
Bitcoin acceptance grows... as does the number of troubling hacks and scams associated with the currency. The Bitcoin community expands via several important new institutions such as Bitcoin Magazine, Coinbase, The Bitcoin Foundation, and Local Bitcoins.

February 11, 2012
Canada-based Bitcoin exchange Paxam ceases all Bitcoin-related activities, claiming to have been forced to do so by "new bank regulations".

February 13, 2012
TradeHill, the world's second largest Bitcoin exchange after Mt. Gox, shuts down after losing $100,000 in a dispute with a payment processor. Tradehill's bank, Internet Archive Federal

Credit Union (IAFCU), seeks to clarify issues regarding its own regulatory and operating standards, and Tradehill's CEO claims it can no longer operate with the bank.

February 27, 2012
Bitcoin Magazine is launched by Vitalik Buterin and Mihai Alisie. Its first edition debuts in May 2012. Bitcoin Magazine provides real-time market info on the exchange rate of Bitcoin against the US dollar, as well as investment guides and articles on using Bitcoin. The periodical circulates both in both online and print formats.

March 1, 2012
The Bitcoinica trading market is hacked. The hacker accesses a wallet containing over 43,000 BTC, worth upwards of $220,000. Bitcoinica announces that it will cover the cost of the hack so that users are not affected and will still be able to access their funds.

March 5, 2012
TradeHill sues the financial transfer service Dwolla. Less than one month prior to this, TradeHill had ceased operating, largely because it lost over $100,000 to a payment processor. The payment processor was not named but is speculated to be Dwolla. The lawsuit seeks two million dollars in compensation for damages.

April 24, 2012
Eric Voorhees launches SatoshiDice, a Bitcoin gambling service. The service operates in defiance of US Laws against gambling. Users place bets by sending BTC to one of several Bitcoin addresses, each with different odds of winning. Bets are made without the need for gamblers to access a website or run client software other than a Bitcoin wallet. Payouts occur almost immediately. The number of low-fee transactions generated by the service leads some to label it an attack on the Bitcoin network.

May 11, 2012
Bitcoinica is hacked again, this time for over 18,000 Bitcoins, worth over $92,000. Bitcoinica ceases trading and promises to refund 50% of customer funds. The refund never materializes.

June 2012
Jeremias Kangas creates the startup LocalBitcoins. Rather than performing transactions through an online exchange, LocalBitcoins allows users to post advertisements for rates at which they would make in-person transactions locally. Users then meet to perform the exchange using cash or another mutually agreed-upon payment method. LocalBitcoins would grow to become a key part of the Bitcoin ecosystem.

June 20, 2012
Coinbase is established by Brian Armstrong and Fred Ehrsam as a platform where users can exchange Bitcoin for fiat currency. Like LocalBitcoins above, Coinbase is significant in that it would grow to become a major part of the ecosystem.

August 17, 2012
Bitcoin Savings and Trust halts interest payments. It officially defaults on August 29th. The owner, Trendon "Pirate40" Shavers, vanishes with 140,000 BTC.

September 4, 2012
Bitcoin exchange BitFloor shuts down after a hacker accesses their Bitcoin wallet and steals almost all the BTC it contains, over 24,000.

September 27, 2012
The Bitcoin Foundation is officially launched, with the mission to "standardize, protect and promote the use of Bitcoin cryptographic money for the benefit of users worldwide." This is not a move to centralize Bitcoin but rather to allow it to continue to operate in a decentralized, peer-to-peer manner through

education and policy initiatives. The original board includes several names who would become famous (or infamous), such as Charlie Shrem (BitInstant) and Mark Karpelès (MtGox).

November 15, 2012
Wordpress, preeminent blog host and provider of popular blogging software, begins accepting bitcoin payments. The Bitcoin community celebrates this as a major development.

November 28, 2012
The first "Halving Day." The number of BTC generated as a "reward" to miners who successfully write a block of transactions to the blockchain is reduced by half, from 50 to 25. This decrease is part of Satoshi Nakamoto's original design to limit the total number of Bitcoins in circulation.

Chapter 6: 2013- The Rise and Fall of Bitcoin

Price of BTC on January 1, 2013: $13.30

More legal challenges loom, including the FBI investigation of the Silk Road and the US Government's seizure of Bitcoin assets connected to Mt. Gox. These events prove that, while Bitcoin is not regulated by the government, crimes committed using Bitcoin are still punishable to the full extent of the law. This is comforting to many who view it as a key step toward going mainstream. They appear to be right; Bitcoin becomes increasingly associated with more legitimate activities and mainstream purchases of consumer goods.

January 25, 2013

Shaun Bridges, a federal investigator tasked with cracking the Silk Road website, speaks with Silk Road moderator Curtis Green. Green agrees to cooperate and gave Bridges and his colleagues information for how to log into Silk Road's user accounts. Within hours, significant thefts from Silk Road are reported and attributed to Curtis Green. However, they are later found to be the work of agent Shaun Bridges.

March 11, 2013
Bitcoin developers inadvertently release a version of the Bitcoin client that is incompatible with prior versions. This causes a fork in the blockchain, with miners and users who did not upgrade to the new version existing on a separate chain from those who upgraded. Users on the "upgraded" chain are forced to downgrade to a previous version of Bitcoin, which causes some miners to lose profits earned on the new chain. This is a serious blow the confidence and price of Bitcoin, however the impact on both is short-lived. After a dip, the price resumes its upward climb.

March 25, 2013
To end an ongoing financial crisis, the island nation of Cyprus accepts a bailout of 10 billion Euros from the European Central Bank. The conditions of the bailout include a "bail-in," or levy collected from private bank accounts with balances over 100,000 Euros. Investors from several foreign nations begin buying other assets (including bitcoin) in an attempt to escape the levy. This spike in demand drives the price of BTC up sharply in the coming month.

April 18, 2013
The value of BTC rises from $93 to $104, passing the $100 mark. The value of bitcoin had been rising steadily in the weeks leading up to this, with some days seeing percentage increases in the double digits.

April 23, 2013
Adam B. Levine launches the "Let's Talk Bitcoin" podcast, featuring himself, Andreas Antonopoulos, and Dr. Stephanie Murphy. The podcast becomes a network of multiple shows focused on various aspects of cryptocurrency. The original LTB

podcast is still produced with the original cast in 2017. The LTB website is a major hub for Bitcoin media.

May 2, 2013
Bitcoin exchange platform CoinLab files a $75 breach of contract lawsuit against Mt. Gox. The two companies had signed a contract asserting that CoinLab would take over all of Mt. Gox's North American transactions.

May 15, 2013
Department of Homeland Security issues warrant against Mt. Gox. The warrant alleges, amongst other things, that Mt. Gox's payment processor Dwolla is unlicensed and operating illegally. The Department of Homeland Security will seize over five million dollars from Dwolla.

July 2, 2013
Internet entrepreneurs Cameron and Tyler Winklevoss file a proposal with the SEC stating their intent to create a Bitcoin ETF.

September 9, 2013
Bitcoin enthusiast Jason King announces plans to build a nine-acre sanctuary for the homeless in Pensacola, Florida. The sanctuary, Satoshi Forest, is funded by bitcoin donations made directly to the bank that holds the mortgage. King will go on to become an outspoken activist and advocate for the homeless. His charity, Sean's Outpost, accepts bitcoin donations exclusively.

October 2013
Bitcoin exchange Circle is launched by entrepreneurs Jeremy Allaire and Sean Neville.

October 2, 2013
Ross Ulbricht, the creator of the Silk Road, is arrested and charged with trafficking of narcotics, money laundering, and other crimes. The US government seizes $3.6 million worth of bitcoin.

October 11, 2013

Payment processor Dwolla announces that as of October 28, 2013 it will no longer process transactions related to virtual currencies, including Bitcoin. Dwolla claims the virtual currency clientele was so small that continuing to accept virtual currencies would impede its plans for growth in other areas. Prior to Dwolla's closure it was one of the few companies that enabled people access to Bitcoin markets and exchanges such as TradeHill.

October 23, 2013

Online wallet service inputs.io is hacked for the first of what will be two hacks within a one-week period. The hacks will lead to a loss of $1.2 million. The operator of the wallet, known as TradeFortress, does not notify clients of the security breach for two weeks. Partial refunds are issued to clients. TradeFortress warns people away from using online wallet services.

October 29, 2013

The first Bitcoin ATM goes online in downtown Vancouver at a Waves coffee shop. The machine allows users to exchange cash for BTC and vice-versa.

November 17, 2013

Payment processor and online wallet BIPS is hacked and relieved of 1295 BTC. BIPS does not issue refunds clients who lost money and attempts to continue functioning.

November 18, 2013

The value of Bitcoin breaks $500, rising by nearly 24%, from $461 to $590.

November 21, 2013

The Cypriot University of Nicosia becomes the first university in the world to accept bitcoin as payment for tuition in a move the school called the Digital Currency Initiative.

November 28, 2013
The value of bitcoin passes $1000 just ten days after reaching $500.

November 29, 2013
Bitcoin reaches $1242 on MtGox. This is the height of the Bitcoin Bubble (some say it is the Third Bitcoin Bubble, counting previous spikes in 2011 and in April of 2013). The BTC price will decline significantly from this point, and will not reach this level again until 2017.
The Bitcoin community celebrates its first Bitcoin Black Friday, highlighting merchants that accept the virtual currency.
Bitcoin "stock exchange" Picostocks is hacked for just under 6000 BTC.

December 2, 2013
Sheep Marketplace, a Bitcoin-driven darknet market styled as a successor to Silk Road, announces that a vendor has absconded with 5400 BTC ($6 million USD). Users identify an even larger number of bitcoins, almost 40,000 being transferred on the blockchain, after which Sheep Marketplace shuts down. Users attempt to track the movement of the stolen BTC on the blockchain for several days before realizing they were following the wrong funds. In May of 2016, Nathan Gibson and Sean Mackert will be arrested for the heist after depositing stolen bitcoin into an account at Coinbase, which routinely verifies the source of deposited funds.

December 5, 2013
China's central bank, the Bank of China, bans any transactions using Bitcoin.

December 8, 2013
Dogecoin, a meme-inspired derivative of Bitcoin, debuts. Doge goes on to develop its own cult following of enthusiasts devoted to the currency.

December 17, 2013
Bitcoin is mentioned in an episode of the Fox TV science fiction show Almost Human.
Business Insider magazine publishes an article by Mark Williams, professor of banking, finance and capital markets at Boston University, in which Williams famously predicts that the price of bitcoin, currently $640, will be below $10 by mid-2014. Despite the current downward trend, Williams is mocked and jeered by the Bitcoin community which dubs him "Professor Bitcorn". A crash in BTC price does occur in 2014, but the price remains an order of magnitude higher than William's prediction.

December 18, 2013
BitcoinTalk user GameKyuubi makes a rambling drunken post entitled "I AM HODLING", which shouts the virtues of holding BTC in the midst of the current sharp downtrend in price. His misspelled admonition to "HODL" becomes an internet meme and remains the most popular Bitcoin meme to date. In hindsight, GameKyuubi's advice turns out to have been correct.

Chapter 7: 2014- Life After "Death"

Price of BTC on January 1, 2014: $770.44

Despite rising interest by merchants and the commercial sector, Bitcoin experiences a crash brought on by, among other things, the collapse of one of its oldest and largest institutions. Despite many announcements of its demise, Bitcoin refuses to die.

January 27, 2014

Charlie Shrem, the CEO and co-founder of BitInstant is arrested for conspiracy to commit money laundering. Shrem will be convicted and sentenced to two years in prison.

February 7, 2014

Mt. Gox halts withdrawals of BTC by its clients, claiming it needs to review its financial processes and fix possible bugs in the software. Unknown by most at this point, Mt. Gox is insolvent due to an ongoing theft that had been occurring since 2011 leading to the loss of over 700,000 BTC. The next day, the value of bitcoin drops from $720 to $690.

In separate undercover stings, two Florida localbitcoin users are arrested for violating Florida anti money-laundering laws and operating unlicensed transmission businesses. Both were converting large numbers of high-dollar transactions of dollars to BTC. Although there will be similar arrests in the future, the large-scale prosecution of Bitcoin users does not materialize as some in the Bitcoin community fear.

February 17, 2014
Mt. Gox issues a press release regarding the security and regulatory concerns it claims to be addressing before it can reinstate BTC withdrawals. CEO Mark Karpelès does not state when clients would once again have access to their funds.

February 20, 2014
Mt. Gox moves its offices to another district in Tokyo due to constant protesting outside of the original site.

Benjamin J. Lawsky, Superintendent of the NY Dept of Financial Services, hosts a question-and-answer session on Reddit's r/Bitcoin forum. Lawsky is a key figure in ongoing work to establish rules for Bitcoin and other virtual currencies. The session's purpose is to answer questions and solicit opinions from the Bitcoin community about upcoming regulation.

February 23, 2014
MtGox CEO Mark Karpelès resigns. Mt. Gox ceases all trading activities, and within a few hours, the website is offline.

February 24, 2014
Entrepreneur Danny Brewster opens Neo & Bee, a Bitcoin bank and payment processor service in Cyprus. The opening of the first branch comes after an extremely aggressive advertising campaign and a round of crowdfunding that raised 9800 BTC. One month later, citing safety concerns, Brewster flees the country with the remainder of the unspent BTC, leaving

employees and vendors unpaid. The Cypriot police issue an arrest warrant, and Brewster remains in hiding (presumably in the UK) until early 2016.

February 28, 2014
Mt. Gox files for Japanese bankruptcy protection, with losses of $473 million.

March 2, 2014
Flexcoin, a Canadian online wallet founded in 2011, is hacked, resulting in the theft of 892 BTC. Users are not reimbursed. Flexcoin shuts down.

March 6, 2014
Newsweek claims they have identified Bitcoin's creator as Dorian Nakamoto, an unemployed engineer in California. Dorian Nakamoto denies the allegations. The next day, a long-dormant P2PFoundation account used by Satoshi Nakamoto in the past posts its first new message in five years stating simply: "I am not Dorian Nakamoto".

March 9, 2014
Hackers leak Mt. Gox's database to the public, exposing the trading activities and account balances of the entire user base. Analysis of the data reveals suspected price manipulation by trading bots.
Also on this day, Mt. Gox files for bankruptcy protection in the US to protect it from US-based clients and creditors.

March 11, 2014
CryptoRush, an altcoin exchange, is hacked, resulting in the loss of 950 BTC and unknown amounts of other cryptocurrencies. CryptoRush attempts to hide the theft and not only continue functioning, but launch their own altcoin. After subsequent hacks lead to massive losses of other altcoins, they shut down.

March 25, 2014
Internal Revenue Service declares that bitcoin will be taxed as property. This move falls short of recognizing bitcoin as currency but is a major step in regulating the booming Bitcoin economy. Amongst other things, the move means that any wages paid in bitcoin had to be reported as taxable income.

April 10, 2014
The People's Bank of China orders the bank accounts of Chinese Bitcoin exchanges be closed by April 15. Despite the loss of bank accounts, some Chinese exchanges continue to function after the deadline.

June 13, 2014
A single mining collective known as Ghash.io officially controls 51% of the Bitcoin network's mining power. This is not a scam or a hack, but rather a natural consequence of Ghash.io's popularity in the fast-growing Bitcoin mining ecosystem. Nevertheless, their control of the majority of mining power (or "hashrate") raises red flags, as this would allow them to reverse transactions and damage the Bitcoin network. Ghash.io acts to divest itself of its majority by asking miners to move to other pools.

June 27, 2014
In the first of several auctions, the U.S. Marshal's Service auctions off nearly 30,000 BTC previously seized in the raid of the Silk Road. Venture capitalist Tim Draper wins the auction at an undisclosed price.

July 18, 2014
Major computer distributer Dell begins accepting bitcoin.

July 23, 2014

The State of New York issues a draft of proposed legislation requiring businesses to obtain a license before being able to accept virtual currencies. The license, referred to as a "bitlicense," will cost $5000 in initial fees and would be required by any company that accepted, stored, or otherwise engaged in business ventures involving Bitcoin. However, some companies that actually apply for the license state the total cost, including legal fees, is closer to $10,000.

September 8, 2014
Payment processor Braintree, a subsidiary of Paypal, begins accepting bitcoin. Merchants that use Braintree for payments now have the option to accept BTC for goods and services.

October 14, 2014
Cryptocurrency exchange Mintpal shuts down unexpectedly. Owner Alex Green, (aka. Ryan Kennedy) disappears with 3894 BTC. Authorities will arrest Green/Kennedy for rape in 2016. No charges will be filed for the cryptocurrency theft.

November 6, 2014
Trendon Shavers, aka "Pirate40" is arrested for his fraudulent Bitcoin Savings and Trust scam. Shavers insists that since bitcoin is not a "security" and not regulated by the US government, his actions were not illegal and do not come under the purview of the Securities and Exchange Commission. Shavers will be imprisoned for 18 months and forced to repay the losses.

November 12, 2014
Reddit user qwsazxcde1, exuberant about a sudden upward spike in price (to $502), makes a celebratory comment entitled "This Is Gentlemen." The omission of the word "it" in the title catches the mischievous eye of the community, which promptly turns the phrase into a meme similar to "HODL" from the previous year. "This is Gentlemen" even finds limited use out site the Bitcoin community as an expression of appreciation.

December 11, 2014
Microsoft begins accepting bitcoin for digital goods. Microsoft executive Eric Lockhard releases the following statement: "The use of digital currencies such as Bitcoin, while not yet mainstream, is growing beyond the early enthusiasts. We expect this growth to continue and allowing people to use Bitcoin to purchase our products and services now allows us to be at the front edge of that trend."

Chapter 8: 2015- Contention and Legitimacy

Price of BTC on January 1, 2015: $313.92
The regulators arrive. The Bitcoin civil war begins. Famous (and infamous) names from previous years resurface in court proceedings while governments make declarations on Bitcoin's legal standing.

January 4, 2015
Popular exchange Bitstamp is hacked. Hackers steal 18,800 BTC from Bitstamp's wallet, but do not steal any customer funds. Bitstamp shuts down for eight days.

March 18, 2015
Shaun Bridges, the corrupt federal agent who simultaneously investigated and exploited the Silk Road website for his own gain, is suspended.

May 19, 2015
Ross Ulbricht, of Silk Road fame, is sentenced to life in prison without parole after being convicted of money laundering, computer hacking, and conspiracy to traffic narcotics.

June 4, 2015
Popular Bitcoin exchange Coinbase stops doing business in Wyoming, claiming regulations make doing business there impractical.

July 1, 2015
Shaun Bridges of the US Secret Service and Carl Force of the Drug Enforcement Agency both plead guilty to charges related to their activities while investigating the Silk Road website. Bridges faces sentencing for theft, money laundering and obstruction of justice. In addition to similar charges, Force plead guilty to extorting Ross Ulbricht.

July 30, 2015
Ethereum, a crypto-platform with advanced scripting and smart contract functionality is launched by a team of developers. Although not directly connected to Bitcoin, Ethereum runs a similar blockchain architecture and one of Ethereum's developers, Vitalik Buterin, is a former Bitcoin developer and co-founder of Bitcoin Magazine.

August 1, 2015
Former MtGox CEO Mark Karpelès is arrested in Japan for fraud and embezzlement.

August 8, 2015
New York implements the bitlicense what was announced the previous year. This is the first time that a US-based government would attempt to regulate virtual currency. As a result of the measure, at least a dozen Bitcoin-based operators decline to do business in New York or service customers in the state. By 2017,

only three companies will have been granted a bitlicense, although many more have applied.

August 15, 2015

Bitcoin Developers Mike Hearn and Gavin Andresen release Bitcoin XT, a new version of the standard Bitcoin Core client that allows for larger block sizes that increase over time as needed. The debate over block size and the constraint it places on Bitcoin scalability has been ongoing for many months prior to this release, with some in the Bitcoin community favoring an increase in block size and others seeking to address it with off-blockchain transactions or other mechanisms. Bitcoin XT is not a fork of the Bitcoin blockchain; it is a fork of the main Bitcoin Core software. Bitcoin Core has a block size of 1MB. Bitcoin XT phases in block size increases every other year beginning when the software is adopted by 75% of the miners. Bitcoin XT fails to gain sufficient support, and the philosophical debate over scaling mechanisms continues. Members of the community and press half-jokingly refer to the contentious and often vitriolic debate over block size as the Bitcoin Civil War.

August 30, 2015

London-based Barclays Bank announces that towards the end of the year it would begin accepting bitcoin for charity donations. The move is part of a strategy to reduce the bank's infrastructure costs.

September 18, 2015

The US Commodities Future Trading Commission declares that bitcoin is a commodity, similar to any consumer good, and therefore under the purview of the Commodity Exchange Act. This move falls short of recognizing bitcoin as money and is considered a blatant step by the US government towards regulating it.

September 22, 2015

Bitcoin exchange Circle becomes the first company to receive a New York bitlicense, which allows it to operate in the State of New York under the new regulatory requirements. Circle initially threatened to join other Bitcoin-based financial operators in a boycott, but reversed its stance and decided to apply for the license.

October 8, 2015
Cameron and Tyler Winklevoss open their own Bitcoin exchange, Gemini, which offers FDIC insurance and licensure in 26 states. This exchange targets traditional individual and institutional investors.

October 22, 2015
The European Union declares that bitcoin and other virtual currencies can be exchanged without VAT, giving it the same legal standing as traditional fiat currency. The move gives the currency an opportunity for sizeable growth in European markets.

October 31, 2015
British-based periodical The Economist features Bitcoin as its cover story, "The Trust Machine." The article highlights the stability in the value of bitcoin over the previous year -- approximately $250 per BTC -- and advocates the potential of the peer-to-peer blockchain technology behind Bitcoin.

November 5, 2015
The US Marshals service auctions off the last of the bitcoin (44,341 BTC) seized from Ross Ulbricht/Silk Road

December 1, 2015
The US Securities and Exchange Commission declares Bitcoin mining companies GAWMiners and ZenMiner to be Ponzi schemes. Both companies, and their associated cryptocurrency Paycoin, were founded by Joshua Garza to share the profits made by mining, however, his computers did not have enough

processing power to back his claims, leading the SEC to recognize his activities as fraudulent.

December 8, 2015

Wired magazine publishes and article claiming Australian programmer and businessman Craig Wright is Satoshi Nakamoto. They base their claim on "leaked documents" that are not produced for confirmation. Shortly after publication, Craig Wright disappears from the internet.

Chapter 9: 2016- Preparing for Launch

Price of BTC on January 1, 2016: $434.46
A year of mostly positive developments lays the groundwork for another meteoric rise. The debate over block size (and control over Bitcoin) continues.

January 2016
Bitcoin Unlimited, another fork of the Bitcoin Core client, is released. Like Bitcoin XT, this fork attempts to address the much-debated block size limit. This version of the Bitcoin software does not have a hard-coded limit, instead allowing users to set their own limit with the expectation that a consensus will eventually be reached. Bugs plague Bitcoin Unlimited after release. In early 2017 only 11% of Bitcoin nodes run Bitcoin Unlimited.

January 14, 2016

Mike Hearn, former Google developer co-creator of Bitcoin XT, makes a vocal exit from Bitcoin, claiming Bitcoin is failing in its mission of being a peer-to-peer digital currency. Hearn's criticisms mostly spring from the lack of an effective solution to capacity scaling, and from the increasing centralization of Bitcoin mining (mostly in China). The Bitcoin community responds with mockery, calling his exit the "Hearnia".

February 10, 2016
Bitcoin Classic, a third fork of Bitcoin Core is released. Bitcoin Classic proposes a single increase to the block size from 1MB to 2MB followed by a democratic process to decide on future changes. As with the other two forks (Bitcoin XT and Bitcoin Unlimited) Bitcoin Classic falls short of the level of adoption necessary to push its implementation across the main Bitcoin network.

March 2016
Japan passes several laws recognizing the legitimacy of virtual currencies such as bitcoin.

April 4, 2016
Bitcoin-powered Online marketplace OpenBazaar launches. True to the peer-to-peer goal of Bitcoin, Open Bazaar allows any person to open an online store and sell items without interference or fees associated with third parties.

April 6, 2016
Bitcoin exchange company Circle becomes the first company to receive the British virtual currency license. The license allows Circle to do business with Barclay's, the British bank that became the first major high street bank to recognize BTC as currency. This event signals changes underway in the British financial marketplace and sets a precedent for future Bitcoin companies that want to expand their businesses in the United Kingdom.

April 27, 2016
Popular PC gaming service Steam begins accepting bitcoin.

May 2, 2016
Craig Wright, outed as Satoshi Nakamoto in a Wired article the previous year, resurfaces and admits that he is, in fact, Satoshi. He attempts to prove the claim by using a private key known to have been associated with Nakamoto in the past. Bitcoin Developer Gavin Andresen supports the claim, but admits he was fooled when the supposed "proof" is scrutinized and summarily dismissed by the Bitcoin community as fraudulent. Payment processor BitPay announces their prepaid Visa card, a debit card that can be loaded with bitcoin. BTC will be converted to USD at the time the card is loaded.

July 9, 2016
The second "Halving Day." The number of bitcoins produced from mining a single block decreases by half, from 25 to 12.5. Prior to the halving, 16,384,950 bitcoins were in circulation, totaling approximately 78% of the maximum.

July 13, 2016
Researchers publish a scholarly report entitled "The Evolution of the Bitcoin Economy: Extracting and Analyzing the Network of Payment Relationships." This paper shows that as of November 2013, Bitcoin has moved beyond being used largely for "sin" activities (drugs, gambling, etc) and onto a stable, legitimate phase in its development in which it was being used for traditional commercial purchases, such as real estate and consumer goods.

August 2, 2016
Bitcoin exchange Bitfinex is hacked, with $72 million worth of BTC stolen. This security breach, the largest since MtGox, sparks a stunning (though brief) 20% drop in price.

October 27, 2016

The national railway operator for Switzerland, SBB, announces that customers will be able to purchase or exchange bitcoin using Swiss francs on their ticketing kiosks. This creates a vast network of over 1000 Bitcoin ATMs.

Also on this day, journalist Kyle Torpey tweets that Barclay's Bank, the first British bank to accept bitcoin, closed down a customer's account because he dealt in the cryptocurrency. This followed several other account closures, seemingly for the same reason. However, the bank continues to advocate for the use of blockchain technology.

December 7, 2016

Bitcoin exchange Circle announces it will cease operating as a Bitcoin exchange and instead focus on a new mobile messaging app that would enable clients to send money within a conversation. This surprise move is seen by some as a precautionary measure that would enable the company to remain solvent in case Bitcoin were to fail.

Chapter 10: 2017- Liftoff

Price of BTC on January 1, 2017: $1005.42
Bitcoin bounces back: The price of BTC in USD surpasses the
high set in the 2013 bubble. The final(?) fate of the long-awaited
ETF is revealed. The past meets the future.

January 1, 2017
Bitcoin breaks the $1000 ceiling which had remained intact
since the bubble of November 2013.

February 1, 2017
The Central Bank of the United Arab Emirates clarifies their
stance on Bitcoin, stating that the cryptocurrency is not illegal.
Regulations released in January lead many to believe the UAE
was outlawing Bitcoin, but this follow-up statement confirms
that Bitcoin is except from those regulations.

February 27, 2017

Bitcoin exchange Coinbase stops servicing customers in Hawaii, stating that the state's regulatory requirements are too heavy a burden on their operations.

March 10, 2017
The Securities and Exchange Commission denies an application filed by Cameron and Tyler Winklevoss for their ETF, the Winklevoss Bitcoin Trust. The denial causes a temporary 14% dip in the value of BTC.

March 29, 2017
Securities and Exchange Commission denies the second application for the Winklevoss Bitcoin Trust. In its decision, the SEC cites the lack of regulation surrounding Bitcoin.

April 2017
Russian lawmakers announce that their longstanding opposition to Bitcoin may change as it may soon become accepted as legitimate currency. The move by the Kremlin aims to help the Russian government regulate Bitcoin and prosecute individuals engaged in money laundering and other fraudulent financial activity.

April 1, 2017
On this day, the Cabinet of Japan's recognition of the bitcoin's as legal currency goes into effect. The Japanese yen provides the second-largest global market for Bitcoin.

April 20, 2017
While not yet an official proclamation, the government of India states their intention to grant legal status to Bitcoin. The details of exactly what this entails are not yet known.

May 9, 2017
Australian Department of the Treasury announces it is eliminating the goods-and-services tax (GST) on bitcoin

purchases in order to "make it easier for new innovative digital currency businesses to operate in Australia".

May 10, 2017
The largest online retailer in Russia, Ulmart, announces it will begin accepting bitcoin payments in September of this year.

May 20, 2017
Bitcoin reaches $2000, having doubled in value since the beginning of the year.

June 7, 2017
The governor of New Hampshire signs a bill that will exempt Bitcoin and other cryptocurrencies from the state's money transmission regulations. Similar regulations have been used to impede Bitcoin businesses and arrest Bitcoin traders in other states.

June 11, 2017
Bitcoin briefly crosses $3000, reaching $3018.54 before dropping to $2682.

June 28, 2017
Burger King announces that stores in Russia will begin accepting bitcoin before the end of the year.

June 30, 2017
The present (or "very recent past"). The Bitcoin price as of this writing is $2521.

The Future...?

Author's Notes: "I Remember..."

I became aware of this new "thing" called Bitcoin sometime prior to 2011. I don't recall the date or circumstance of my first exposure, but I remember listening to the February 9, 2011 Security Now podcast and being impressed that host Steve Gibson had such a positive opinion of Bitcoin. Although I had heard of it before, I didn't take Bitcoin seriously until after that point. I have been a silent observer and participant in the Bitcoin phenomenon ever since. The timeline you've just read is more than just dates and events to me. As someone who actually witnessed these events as they unfolded, this book is a personal history.

I remember skipping lunch one day so I could walk to the bank and complete my first BitInstant purchase. The "instant" portion of the name turned out not to be true. I was terrified that I'd been scammed, but I got my BTC a few hours later. I still own a tiny amount of BTC from this early purchase.

I remember making the awkward and expensive series of exchanges between Dwolla and Tradehill that was necessary to buy BTC online. I remember having mixed feelings about Dwolla abandoning cryptocurrency and Tradehill shutting down. I used them both, but I thought they needed to make room for something easier.

I remember playing SatoshiDice exactly once. I remember thinking it was going to make someone a lot of money. But not necessarily the players. I guess I wasn't the target audience.

I remember using MtGox. I also remember abandoning the platform well before the ship began to sink. This timeline implies that MtGox's collapse was sudden and unexpected, but there were many, many warning signs that a lot of otherwise intelligent people chose to ignore.

I remember my first and only visit to the Silk Road, terrified that the FBI and DEA were going to label me a "person of interest" just for browsing. I didn't purchase anything. I remember following the Ulbricht case with increasing dismay and snickering at the so-called "successors" to the Silk Road that turned out to be little more than scams. I remember the launch of OpenBazaar, and I'm still waiting for it to get the attention it deserves. Please check it out at www.openbazaar.org. (I am in no way associated with the project.)

I remember dipping my toe into altcoin trading... attempting to make money buying/selling cryptocurrencies I had no real knowledge of or interest in. I gave up in disgust long before the exchange disappeared with everyone's money. I don't even remember which exchange it was.

I remember my sleepless exuberance during the great Bitcoin Bubble of 2013. I remember trying to calculate the exact BTC price that would qualify as a "life-changing" amount of money. The bubble burst well short of the number I came up with. I was shocked. I remember seeing the suicide hotline posts on Reddit and wondering if things were really that bad. For some people, they were. Think about that for a moment.

I remember the Cyprus "bail-in", and how it made people who couldn't find Cyprus on a map the day before suddenly start paying attention. Eliminating middle-men and third parties (like banks and governments) from our finances was a goal of the cypherpunk movement that inspired Bitcoin. Bitcoin is how. Cyprus is WHY. Everyone thinks "It Can't Happen Here" until it does. The Cypriot people thought that. Think about that for a moment, too.

I remember cheering at "I Am Not Dorian Nakamoto". YES!

I remember all the hacks and all the scams. I put a tiny bit of BTC in Bitcoin Savings and Trust "just because". It was almost certainly a Ponzi scheme... but what if it wasn't? I smiled when I lost my money. I'd just been proven right, after all. I Told Me So! Bitcoin was the "Wild West"... a brand new financial infrastructure built and maintained by rank amateurs with zero oversight. I remember nobody having a problem with that... until suddenly they did.

I remember my disillusionment after the bubble. I watched Bitcoin with waning enthusiasm for a year... waiting for the next bubble... before deciding I was just going to stop paying attention. If Bitcoin was going to make me rich it would do so without my interest or participation. I was done. Despite my promise to myself, I still watched Bitcoin... just not as closely. I couldn't help myself. I avoided learning the BTC price for as long as possible though. It turned out to be easier than I thought. There are more important things in life than Bitcoin. Once you finish this book, you should probably spend some time with your family. I sure am.

I remember wondering just what the big deal was with Dogecoin. I still don't know. I remember wondering the same thing about Ethereum, but I know the answer to that one. I think I know what my next book is going to be about.

I remember cringing as someone I respected (and still do) detailed their involvement (and lack thereof) in the Neo & Bee debacle. Now, years later, it seems like I'm the only person that remembers Neo and Bee.

I remember the release of Bitcoin XT and the start of the so-called civil war. This was during the time when I wasn't paying much attention, so I remember being confused as to just what the hell was going on. It turned out to be a bigger deal than I first thought. Was the American Civil War fought over slavery, or was it fought over state's rights? The answer is "Yes". Was the Bitcoin civil war fought over the single issue of scalability, or over control of the code? The answer is the same.

I don't remember "HODL", but I do remember "This Is Gentlemen!". I watched a meme being born. I don't know why that makes me smile so much, but it does.

I remember using Bitcoin to buy video games on Steam last week. It was notable because it WASN'T notable. No errors. No delays. No frustration. No drama. Easier than a credit card. Almost... but not quite... like cash for the internet.

I remember ALL the times that Bitcoin has "died".

I could go on. No, really, I could. But I think you get the idea. I didn't wax nostalgic above to prove my Bitcoin "cred," but to remind myself and show you how much of a part Bitcoin has played in my life. It did not make me rich. It did not change my career. It did not bankrupt me. But it educated, occupied, and entertained me for over half a decade. And it has paid a few bills here and there. People getting on the Bitcoin train now lack an appreciation for what people like me know, saw, and did. They don't know why we say the things we say, like "HODL" and "Never leave your BTC on an exchange, are you insane!? WTF is wrong with you!?" They don't understand the use of the word "Gox" as a verb, or why there seem to be so many libertarians and anarchists lurking around. It's all in the history. It's all in the timeline. And this final chapter is just my attempt to show just how valuable this knowledge is... even if it's just nostalgia.

And trust me, it's a LOT more than just nostalgia.

I hope you learned something useful. I hope you enjoyed doing so.

Thanks for reading; I'll see you in the next book.

Eric Morse.

A Note on Source Material:

This timeline of public events is compiled from multiple sources, including (but not limited to):

History of Bitcoin: http://historyofbitcoin.org/
Bitcoin Price Chart with Historic Events:
https://99bitcoins.com/price-chart-history/
BitcoinTalk Forum: https://bitcointalk.org/
The R/Bitcoin subreddit: https://www.reddit.com/r/bitcoin
And the author's own memory.